EASY
ALLERGY-
FREE
COOKING

EASY ALLERGY-FREE COOKING

SIMPLE & SAFE EVERYDAY RECIPES FOR EVERYONE

KAYLA CAPPIELLO

Skyhorse Publishing

Skyhorse Publishing books may be purchased in bulk at special discounts for
sales promotion, corporate gifts, fund-raising, or educational purposes. Special
editions can also be created to specifications. For details, contact the Special Sales
Department, Skyhorse Publishing, 307 West 36th Street, 11th Floor, New York,
NY 10018 or info@skyhorsepublishing.com.

Skyhorse® and Skyhorse Publishing® are registered trademarks of Skyhorse
Publishing, Inc.®, a Delaware corporation.

Visit our website at www.skyhorsepublishing.com.

10 9 8 7 6 5 4 3 2 1

Library of Congress Cataloging-in-Publication Data is available on file.

Cover design by David Ter-Avanesyan
Cover photo credit by Kayla Cappiello

Print ISBN: 978-1-5107-7390-5
Ebook ISBN: 978-1-5107-7391-2

Printed in China

Dedicated to the ten-year-old version of me, running to the bathroom,
wondering if her stomach problems will ever get better.

I promise, it gets better.

Contents

Introduction

A few years ago, I was running around, doing whatever I wanted in my mid-twenties, thinking I was invincible. I certainly was not eating healthy and was absolutely pretending it didn't affect me. News flash: this way of living *was* affecting me.

After a fun night out, I was tired, sluggish, and unmotivated. It would take me two days to recover from eating pasta and even longer to recover from drinking beer. Take-out pizza was a staple of my weekend itinerary, and to say I didn't know the damage this way of living was doing to me physically, and mentally, was an understatement.

Gluten? I was eating it with no idea I had the celiac gene.

Cheese? I was inhaling it without a clue I was lactose intolerant.

I was bloated, sick, and my brain was foggy. And to top it off, I had no idea why.

After multiple doctor visits, seemingly never-ending proposed diet changes, and sleepless nights of research, I slowly adjusted my eating habits. I took a deep dive into finding the foods that felt right for me. Eventually, the tests came back positive for the celiac gene, positive for being lactose intolerant, and positive for being allergic to tree nuts (almonds, hazelnuts, and pistachios). Things finally began to make sense. I wasn't crazy. I knew my body. Above all, I knew what did and didn't feel right for me, and I started to trust myself.

I started a journey exploring food that made me feel energized and healthy. I eliminated the food I could not tolerate, and I adjusted recipes to fit my new lifestyle. Around this time, I felt incredibly frustrated that I couldn't find any recipes that worked for my new eating habits. I wanted to find a simple guide for what I could make next, but it wasn't out there. If a recipe was gluten-free, the recipe was made with almond flour, and I was allergic to almonds. If a recipe was dairy-free, recipes still included wheat. I was lost and alone on this food journey with no one I could relate to.

To cope with my frustration, and also to celebrate my little victories, I posted my recipes on my blog. Slowly, people started responding to them. I realized there were others experiencing the same thing; we couldn't find recipes that catered to us. I wanted to give them a voice and provide them with what I hadn't had for myself: a simple guide to eating healthy while living with dietary restrictions.

Eating healthy does not have to be expensive, time-consuming, or unattainable. This cookbook focuses on simple guides for everyone to incorporate healthy eating habits into everyday life, but it will also teach home cooks with allergies that they don't have to miss out on their favorite meals. These recipes focus on providing healthy food substitutions, allergy-friendly options for everyday life, and stocking a pantry full of better ingredients for a wholly healthier lifestyle!

Who am I?

Let's buckle in and time travel together back to 2008, 2009, or maybe even 2010. I was a skinny, awkward, college-aged girl, focused on school and spending time with my friends, the same as anyone else my age. We all ate three meals a day, sometimes a fourth solely because we were hungry—not because we needed nutrients. We drank more alcohol than we should, slept less than we should, studied less than we should, and I wouldn't have known what a healthy lifestyle was if I had tripped over it. If anyone ever tried to tell me that, in a few years, I'd completely refocus my life around cooking healthy food and sharing my allergy stories with thousands of people, I'd have locked them in a holding cell and thrown away the key. *That guy is saying ridiculous things; don't make eye contact with him.*

Back in college, a.k.a. my awkward skinny phase, I was paying no attention to what I was eating, the type of food I was putting into my body, or how much of it I was consuming. I was skinny, which I incorrectly thought meant I was healthy, and I was choosing the fried appetizer sampler at every restaurant I could. Do I regret it? No. Did I know what I was putting my body through, though? Also no.

After a typical college night out, I found myself incredibly tired, sluggish, and extremely unmotivated. I was in a fog. I'd lie in bed all morning, getting up once an hour like clockwork to run to the bathroom, and it wasn't to pee. My stomach would be reeling. I thought, *This is what every college kid goes through.* No one else around me seemed more motivated, so I didn't think I was doing anything wrong. I was running around thinking I was invincible simply because I was young.

Fast-forward to 2013. I was at my first corporate job, boxed in a cubicle, working an entry-level position. I was grabbing lunch every day with my coworkers from whatever deli was our favorite that week. I'd head straight to the sandwich counter like no other option existed. I loved those flat NYC pressed paninis, the semicircle ones with the heavy grill marks. They were my favorite. Turkey paninis, pesto chicken paninis, veggie sandwiches, you name it. I thought I was doing myself a favor. *There isn't a ton of cheese on this, I picked low-fat mayo instead of honey mustard, this only has veggies.* I thought I was making healthy decisions. But why wasn't I feeling better? We'd get back to the office, just in time for the worst hour of the day for me: from 1:00 to 2:00. I would struggle to keep my eyes open; my eyelids felt like twenty-pound weights forcing themselves closed without my consent. I was tired and sluggish, and this was a daily occurrence.

Somewhere around 2018, I got food poisoning. You know when people say *has anyone ever actually gotten salmonella from raw cookie dough or are people trying to stop me from living my life?* Yes, well, I'm here as the poster child to tell you salmonella is, in fact, real. At the time, I had no idea what was wrong with me. I couldn't keep food down and my heart was racing. After the initial sickness subsided, I still didn't feel right and I remember thinking, *When is this going to get better for me?*

Little did I know that not only was I going to get better and get over the salmonella poisoning, but I was actually going to find out what the heck was going on with me.

"You have the celiac gene. You are also lactose intolerant."

As soon as the doctor spoke those words to me it was like finding that last piece of a jigsaw puzzle. I had researched gastroenterologists and made an appointment hoping to solve my stomach sickness issue. After an initial consultation, then a follow-up appointment and numerous tests, I finally had some answers. I did have food poisoning, for which I was prescribed an antibiotic. But, in addition, I found out I had a gluten intolerance and a dairy intolerance.

She explained the symptoms of each problem to me, and I felt like I was checking each and every one of them off as she read down the list.

Symptoms of being lactose intolerant: bloating, diarrhea, indigestion, flatulence, stomach cramps.

Symptoms of celiac disease: bloating, diarrhea, indigestion, flatulence, stomach cramps, fatigue, head "fog."

Check. Check. Check.

I added this to my already long list of tree nut allergies (almonds, hazelnuts, pistachios) and thought, *Is there anyone else out there with my dietary issues? Am I ever going to find a recipe that works for me again?*

Well, I'm here to tell you, YES. If you have any dietary restrictions or food intolerances, yes, you will eat good food again. If you have allergies, yes, you, too, will eat good food again.

What do I keep stocked in my kitchen?

How to lay a healthy foundation with a backstock of foods

I'm a big supporter of laying a solid foundation for eating healthy, and that starts with the things you keep stocked in your kitchen on a regular basis. Having healthy options in stock makes it easy to reach for the healthy option because that is all you have. This healthy stockpile forces you to make the healthy choice every single time. There is no unhealthy food lingering in the corner calling out to you, begging for you to eat it.

How I grocery shop

Someone once told me that if you're going to browse through the grocery store, only browse the outside aisles. That's where all the freshest food is kept. The middle aisles should only be used for things you absolutely need. This stuck with me. The outer path of the grocery store contains the freshest items with the least amount of processed ingredients. Think about it. The outside aisles are produce, meat, fish, fresh eggs, and dairy. The inside items are more processed, such as cereals, canned vegetables, jarred sauces, etc. And while these items are certainly not bad to eat, you don't want to live off them for every single meal you make.

Healthy grocery shopping list worksheet

On the following page is a sample grocery shopping list that I keep with me at all times. It's a reminder of the items I like to keep my kitchen stocked with. Do I buy all these items every single time I go to the grocery store? No. But at least I know the food I don't want to stray from. At least I can keep myself reminded of the healthy items I like to buy over and over again to lay that healthy foundation in my own kitchen.

Breads:
- ☐ Gluten-free sliced bread
- ☐ Brown rice tortillas
- ☐ Cauliflower crusts
- ☐ Gluten-free pizza crust

Carbs and Grains:
- ☐ Chickpea pasta
- ☐ Lentil pasta
- ☐ Rice (brown or white)
- ☐ Cauliflower rice or vegetable rice
- ☐ Pumpkin puree
- ☐ butternut squash puree
- ☐ sweet potato puree
- ☐ tomato sauce
- ☐ Black beans
- ☐ Chickpeas
- ☐ Gluten-free tater tots or vegetable tots

Oils/Fats/Spreads:
- ☐ Avocado oil
- ☐ Olive oil
- ☐ Light olive oil light oil spray
- ☐ Peanut butter/nut butter/granola butter/tahini

Baking:
- ☐ Gluten-free flour blend
- ☐ Coconut flour
- ☐ Brown-rice flour
- ☐ Baking powder
- ☐ Baking soda
- ☐ Applesauce
- ☐ Cocoa powder
- ☐ Dairy-free chocolate chips

Fruit:
- ☐ Blueberries
- ☐ Strawberries
- ☐ Pineapple

Produce:
- ☐ Arugula
- ☐ Spinach
- ☐ Romaine lettuce
- ☐ Multicolor peppers
- ☐ Red onions
- ☐ White onions
- ☐ Broccoli
- ☐ Brussels sprouts
- ☐ Zucchini
- ☐ Tomatoes

Protein (kept in your refrigerator or freezer):
- ☐ Chicken breasts
- ☐ Ground chicken
- ☐ Ground turkey
- ☐ Sliced turkey
- ☐ Turkey pepperoni
- ☐ Turkey bacon or vegan bacon
- ☐ Chicken sausage or vegan sausage
- ☐ Eggs

Dairy/Non-Dairy:
- ☐ Cheddar (vegan or regular)
- ☐ Mozzarella (vegan or regular)
- ☐ Vegan parmesan
- ☐ Oat milk or other plant-based milk
- ☐ Vegan butter

Potatoes:
- ☐ Sweet potatoes
- ☐ Red potatoes

What can I use as substitutes?

Part 1: Dairy-free/Vegan cheese substitutes

When I started out, the thought of cutting cheese out of my life was insane. Going vegan or dairy-free felt like losing this huge category of food I lived for: pizza, pastas, cheese boards, nachos . . . My long list of cheesy foods have a special place in my heart. But to be completely honest, the transition was easier than I expected once I discovered vegan/dairy-free cheese.

Was this experience a difficult transition? Yes.

Does dairy-free cheese taste the same as dairy cheese? No.

But can this cheese substitute fill the void you might be feeling? Yes.

In place of regular cheese in a recipe or meal, a simple substitute is dairy-free cheese.

Cutting out dairy means cutting out all products that have milk in them. This is more than just cutting out a daily glass of milk. The most common foods that have dairy in them are cheese, ice cream, creams, yogurt, butter, and milk.

The easiest way to find a dairy-free product is to look for products that do not contain milk or dairy products on the nutritional label. If the label says "contains milk," do not consider that product dairy-free. Because milk comes from a cow, vegan products will always be dairy-free. If a product such as cheese is labeled as vegan, you can trust the cheese is dairy-free. Look for vegan butters, vegan cheeses, and vegan milks such as oat milk or soy milk.

There are lactose-free cheeses, nut cheeses, oat cheeses, coconut cheeses, and I found them to be dizzying to navigate through them. I can't stress this enough: putting in the research to taste test and find the ones that work for you is key. Check out the ingredient list and buy a few brands that work for you, then spend some time comparing them.

When I first made the transition to dairy-free cheese, I focused on shredded cheese options first and made some notes about what I liked and what I didn't like. I gave the dairy-free cheese a ranking and moved on to the next. The chart made it easy to figure out the best option for me, so I wouldn't try a brand I did not like more than once by mistake.

Beet, Goat Cheese, and Caramelized Onion Pizza, page 170

Your Cheese Ranking Worksheet

Brand	Cheesy Flavor	Positives	Negatives	Ranking
Add brand here	*Cheddar*	*Melts well. Good for pizzas and pastas.*	*Too creamy. Didn't like the taste when it wasn't melted*	*7/10*

"Cheesy" products to always have on hand:

- Vegan parmesan cheese
  Look for options made from potato starch and coconut. Make sure to avoid nut cheese if you are tree nut–free like me! This is used in cheese sauces, vegan dishes, and sprinkled on pasta, veggies, pizza, etc.

- Nutritional yeast
  This is to simulate a cheesy flavor in sauces when making cheese sauces like vegan mac and cheese and baked pastas.

- Turmeric, paprika, Dijon mustard, garlic powder, onion powder, salt, pepper
  This mixture can also help simulate a cheesy flavor when making vegan dishes such as vegan tofu "eggs."

Part 2: Gluten-free/Nut-free bread and grain substitutes

Along with that long list of cheesy foods I loved came the carbs I loved. Breads? Pastas? Pizzas? Cutting out these things was simply not an option. I set out to find the best alternatives I could. I wanted options that tasted the same, or at least as close to the original taste as I could get. I was on a mission.

Gluten is in a *lot* of foods. Cutting gluten out includes cutting out all products that have wheat, barley, or rye in them. The most common foods with these ingredients are pastas, breads, baked goods, cereals, crackers, soy sauce, some dressings, and some soups.

The easiest way to find gluten-free products is looking for products labeled as gluten-free. That label means the product was safely manufactured and packaged to make sure the food does not contain gluten and that it has no cross contamination. That label is a safe sign that the product is safely gluten-free.

Another place to check is the ingredient list. If the ingredients contain wheat, barley, or rye, or the label says "contains wheat," then the food is not safe.

Pasta

There are all kinds of pasta substitutes out there—lentil, chickpea, gluten-free flour blend pasta. Again, taste test, taste test, taste test.

Lentil pasta

Slight lentil taste but holds its shape well. It's easy to use with sauces and doesn't get mushy. Plus, lentil pasta has the added benefit of lentils cooked right in. Good source of B vitamins, iron, magnesium, potassium zinc, plant-based protein, and fiber.

Chickpea pasta

Good taste but breaks apart easily. To avoid this, I make sure to cook the pasta al dente and pour the sauce on top. When you add the pasta to the sauce and stir, chickpea pasta doesn't hold its shape well. Plus, chickpea pasta has the added health benefit of chickpeas cooked right in. Good source of calcium, magnesium, and fiber.

Gluten-free blended-flour pasta

This pasta is the closest in taste and texture to actual flour pasta because this version is made up of other gluten-free flours blended together. The only downside here is that this pasta might not have the same health benefits of pasta made from lentils or chickpeas or other vegetable-based pastas.

Grains

Cauliflower

Cauliflower is an easy substitute for grains without most of the carbs. Cauliflower can be ground up to make pizza crusts and tortillas or even used as rice. It's extremely versatile and flavorless, so cauliflower will take on the flavors of the recipe itself.

Corn tortillas

A simple hack to keeping gluten-free in Mexican-inspired dishes and tacos is using corn tortillas instead of flour tortillas. They are a little firmer and work better once warmed for 3 to 5 minutes in the oven. They usually come in smaller sizes, so make sure you stock up!

Gluten-free breads

There are so many gluten-free bread options out there for you to choose from. Breads made from brown-rice flour, quinoa flour, tapioca flour, potato starch, amaranth, arrowroot, etc. They come in all different sizes and shapes, from traditional bread to rolls and everything in between. Brown rice four tortillas are easy to find and make wonderfully crispy crusts for simple at-home pizzas.

Gluten-free grains and rice

Grain bowls are one of the easiest recipes to make that inherently do not contain any gluten. Grain bowls can easily be made with white rice, brown rice, or quinoa. If a grain bowl calls for farrow or couscous, that recipe will contain gluten. You can easily substitute white rice, brown rice, quinoa, or even cauliflower rice.

Pizza Crusts

There are a ton of ways to make pizza gluten-free! There are loads of different frozen gluten-free pizza crusts, frozen cauliflower pizza crusts, and gluten-free pizza dough you can buy! You can use brown rice tortillas—they make a great crispy thin crust! You can also use gluten-free pitas to make personal-sized pizzas, gluten-free baguettes to make French bread pizzas, gluten-free bagels to make pizza bagels, or gluten-free toast to make pizza toasts! All of my pizza recipes can be made on any of these crusts! Pick up your crust of choice and follow the recipe for the perfect Friday night fake takeout.

Quick Crusts!

Quick gluten-free brown rice tortilla pizza crust:
Preheat oven to 400°F. Add brown rice tortilla to a lined baking sheet. This will bake quickly! Bake for 2 to 3 minutes until it is slightly browned. Then remove, add toppings, and add back to oven for another 3 to 5 minutes until the crust is crispy and browned along the edges. Because all tortillas are slightly different, some will cook faster than others. Be sure to keep an eye on it to make sure it is not burning. Add extra time to make a crispier crust.

Quick gluten-free pizza bread crust:
Preheat oven to 400°F. Add slices of gluten-free bread to a lined baking sheet. Add toppings and place in oven for 5 to 7 minutes, until the bread is brown and crispy and the cheese is fully melted. Because all gluten-free bread slices are slightly different, some will cook faster than others. Be sure to keep an eye on it to make sure it is not burning. Add extra time to make a crispier crust.

Quick gluten-free pizza bagel crust:
Preheat oven to 400°F. Slice gluten-free bagel in half. Add slices of gluten-free bagel to a lined baking sheet. Add toppings and place in oven for 5 to 7 minutes until the bagel is brown and crispy and the cheese is fully melted. Because all gluten-free bagels are slightly different, some will cook faster than others. Be sure to keep an eye on it to make sure it is not burning. Add extra time to make a crispier crust.

Quick gluten-free French bread pizza crust:
Preheat oven to 400°F. Slice gluten-free baguette in half longways. Open and add both sides to a lined baking sheet, face up. Add toppings and place in oven for 5 to 7 minutes, until the bread is brown and crispy and the cheese is fully melted. Because all gluten-free breads are slightly different, some will cook faster than others. Be sure to keep an eye on it to make sure it is not burning. Add extra time to make a crispier crust.

Part 3: Gluten-free/Vegan meat substitutes

Tofu

Tofu can be an inexpensive and simple option to avoiding meat in any recipe. Tofu can be easily transformed to create a soft egg-like texture and can be air-fried to mimic crispy fried food when covered in sauce (bbq sauce, buffalo sauce, orange sauce, etc.).

Easy Air-Fried Tofu

1 block extra-firm tofu
1 cup plant-based milk
¼ cup gluten-free flour
¼ cup nutritional yeast

Slice the tofu into 1-inch cubes or 1-inch strips. Add the plant-based milk to a bowl. In a separate bowl, add the gluten-free flour and nutritional yeast. Dip the tofu in the milk and then in the flour mixture. Make sure the tofu is evenly covered. Add to the air fryer in a way that avoids overlapping. Air-fry on 390°F for 10 to 12 minutes until the outside coating is browned and crispy!

Tater Tots

Tater tots are a perfect substitute for ground meat. Once diced up and added to a frying pan, tater tots are easy to break apart and crisp up to mimic ground meat, especially in a taco recipe.

Easy Tater Tot Vegan "Meat"

1 cup gluten-free tater tots
½ tablespoon oil of choice

If tater tots are frozen, place in a microwave-safe bowl and warm in increments of 30 seconds until tots are room temperature. Next, crush tater tots with a fork until they are fully ground. The tater tots should be crushed into tiny pieces and should resemble the look of ground meat. In a frying pan, add the crushed tater tots and ½ tablespoon oil of choice. Pan-fry on medium to medium-high heat until the tater tot pieces are of desired crispiness, approximately 7 to 11 minutes.

Cauliflower

Cauliflower is a simple, healthy substitute in recipes when trying to mimic specifically crispy or fried chicken. Once battered and air-fried, use crispy breaded cauliflower on anything from salads, to tacos, to Asian-inspired dishes. Sometimes a healthy veggie substitute is the way to go.

Easy Battered Cauliflower

2 eggs
1 cup gluten-free flour + 1 teaspoon garlic + 1 teaspoon onion powder
2 cups cauliflower florets

Crack 2 eggs into a bowl. Scramble. Add the gluten-free flour, garlic, and onion to a separate bowl. Dip the cauliflower florets in the egg mixture, then the flour mixture. Add to the air fryer, spacing pieces out so none are overlapping. Air-fry on 390°F until the outside coating is browned and crispy!

Part 4: Baking substitutes and healthy hacks

Gluten-Free Flours for Baking

Gluten-free flour

1:1 ratio baking flours are the best. The company has already figured out the correct ratio for you, so it's a simple substitute you barely have to think about. They mimic wheat flour so closely that, if used correctly, you won't even notice the change.

Brown-rice flour

Brown-rice flour is one of my favorites. Brown-rice flour has more nutrients than white-rice flour but still has a neutral taste. Brown-rice flour is ideal to use in both baking and as a thickener in sauces and soups.

Coconut flour

Coconut flour has a slight coconut taste and is used best in conjunction with other flour blends when baking. Coconut flour is not a 1:1 substitute for wheat flour. This flour is a dryer flour and absorbs moisture.

Chickpea flour

This flour is good for breads, crusts, muffins, and cookies. Chickpea flour is ideal for a more neutral base. This flour is a dense flour, so not ideal for recipes that gear toward a fluffy consistency.

Egg Substitutes for Baking

Sometimes eggs are one of the only ingredients in recipes keeping it from being vegan. Cutting out eggs can also make a recipe a healthier option. Below are some substitutes to hacking a recipe to eliminate eggs.

Applesauce:
Use applesauce instead of eggs when baking.
Ratio: 1 egg = ¼ cup of applesauce

Mashed bananas:
Use mashed bananas instead of eggs when baking.
Ratio: 1 egg = ¼ cup of mashed bananas

Pureed pumpkin/sweet potato/butternut squash
Use sweet potato, pumpkin, or butternut squash puree instead of eggs when baking.
Ratio: 1 egg = ¼ cup of sweet potato, pumpkin, or butternut squash

Milk Substitutes for Cooking and Baking

Oat milk

I'm a huge fan of oat milk. Oat milk can be gluten-free-friendly (check to make sure the milk uses certified gluten-free oats if you're buying it!), does not contain any nuts, and does not contain any dairy/lactose. Oat milk has a similar consistency to skim milk. It's a bit thinner than whole milk but can still froth and makes a good, creamy sauce base since this milk has a very neutral flavor. Oat milk is low in fat and high in fiber. Oat milk has a neutral taste but can be found in flavors such as vanilla and chocolate. I most often use plain or unsweetened.

Rice milk

Rice milk is also gluten-free-friendly, does not contain any nuts, and does not contain any dairy/lactose, but is slightly more watery consistency than skim milk. Its taste is muted and neutral. It's thin but can still be used in creamy sauces and baking with adjustments. Rice milk is low in fat.

Soy milk

Soy milk is a great dairy-free, nut-free option. Soy milk has a neutral taste and a creamy consistency. The thickness is similar to cow's milk. I most often use plain or unsweetened.

Flax and seed milks

Flax milk is also gluten-free, nut-free, and dairy-free and can be a great substitute when cooking or baking.

Coconut milk

Coconut milk is a fantastic dairy-free option, especially when baking. But do note, coconut milk does contain more fat and saturated fat than oat or rice milks. It's creamy and sweet and perfect when looking for dairy-free milk to use in a healthy treat.

Butter/Oil Substitutes for Baking

These substitutes can be made to cut out butter and thus make your recipe dairy-free or vegan . . . but also make your baked goods secretly healthier! Butter has so much saturated fat. Incorporating some of these substitutes chips away at an overall healthier lifestyle. Do you want to live a healthy life? Yes. But do you still want chocolate cupcakes? Yes. And is that okay? YES.

Avocado substitute

1 cup butter = 1 cup avocado

1 cup avocado is generally 360 calories, 34 grams fat, but only 4.9 grams saturated fat

1 cup butter is generally 1628 calories, 184 grams fat, and 117 grams saturated fat

Notes: Substituting avocado for butter means overall fewer calories and less saturated fat to keep your overall health and cholesterol in check! Of course, the type of butter you buy will change the nutrition facts, but this is just generic butter to give you an idea of what kind of calories and the amount of fat we are looking at saving!

Avocado oil

1 cup melted butter = 1 cup avocado oil

1 cup avocado oil is generally 1984 calories, 224 grams fat, but only 25.6 grams saturated fat

1 cup butter is generally 1628 calories, 184 grams fat, and 117 grams saturated fat

Notes: Substituting avocado for butter brings some extra calories and only ¼ the amount of saturated fat. Again, nutrition facts vary depending on what brand you are buying, but I'm using generic avocado oil and generic butter as an example to portray how much less fat is in avocado oil than butter.

Vegan butter

1 cup butter = 1 cup vegan butter

Vegan butter is designed to give you as close of a taste to butter as possible. It's a good substitute when baking because vegan butter accomplishes the same goal as natural butter.

Peanut butter + oil

½ cup peanut butter + ½ cup oil = 1 cup butter

The peanut butter and oil combo is a similar consistency to butter but without the dairy or animal byproduct. Choose peanut butter made from only ground peanuts instead of one that is a peanut and oil mix to help make this substitute healthier.

Part 5: Low-carb substitutes

Cauliflower and Vegetable Rice

Since rice is gluten-free, it's really easy to serve rice with every meal as a side dish or a base to a meal. It's absolutely my go-to when I'm looking for something naturally safe to eat that I don't need to think twice about. I eat white rice and brown rice on a weekly basis. But, to help create a lower carb rice option, sub a cauliflower rice, vegetable rice, or lentil rice at a 1:1 ratio in place of white rice or brown rice. If the texture is too different for you, use half white/brown rice and half vegetable rice to get a more traditional "rice-like" texture.

Pork Rind Breadcrumbs

When breading chicken or making something with breadcrumbs such as meatballs, pork rind panko breadcrumbs are a perfect low-carb substitute. You can find seasoned and unseasoned options. They are a perfect 1:1 substitute for breadcrumbs. You can also use half breadcrumbs and half pork rind panko. They get crispy in the air fryer, as well!

Life-Changing Dressings and Condiments

If you're the type of person who eats chicken fingers only because they're craving honey mustard, then this is the chapter for you. I, hands down, choose my meals based on what type of sauce or condiment I'm craving. Whether it be salad dressings, sauces for your chicken fingers, or dips for your french fries, these dressings and condiments will change your life.

Vegan Avocado Crema

Yield: ½ cup

Gluten-free | Nut-free
Options: Dairy-free | Low-fat | Vegan

What you'll need:

½ avocado

1 teaspoon garlic powder

½ teaspoon salt

½ teaspoon pepper

¼ cup yogurt

Dairy-free option: Use dairy-free yogurt

Low-fat option: Use fat-free yogurt or light sour cream

Vegan option: Use vegan greek yogurt

This avocado crema is the perfect vegan creamy topping for tacos or anything with a little kick!

What to do:

In a bowl, add the avocado, garlic, salt, pepper, and yogurt. Mix together until fully blended and smooth. It's okay to use a food processor, if needed. Store in an airtight container in the fridge for 3 to 5 days.

Arugula Pesto Aioli

Yield: ½ cup

Gluten-free
Options: Dairy-free | Low-fat | Vegan

What you'll need:

1 handful arugula

3 tablespoons olive oil

2 tablespoons parmesan cheese

1 tablespoon garlic powder

3 tablespoons cashews or pine nuts

1 tablespoon water

3 tablespoons mayonnaise

½ teaspoon salt

½ teaspoon pepper

Dairy-free option: Use vegan parmesan
  cheese

Low-fat option: Use light mayo

Vegan option: Use vegan parmesan cheese
  and vegan mayo

I love putting this arugula pesto on white pizzas or flatbreads. The arugula gives the aioli some extra nutrients!

What to do:

Add all ingredients to a blender or food processor and blend until fully combined. Do not over-blend. Mixture shouldn't be smooth like a salad dressing; it should resemble a thick paste. Store in an airtight container in the fridge for 3 to 5 days.

Lemon Garlic Aioli

Yield: ½ cup

Gluten-free | Dairy-free | Nut-free
Options: Low-fat | Vegan

What you'll need:

¼ cup mayonnaise

½ tablespoon minced fresh garlic

½ teaspoon avocado oil

½ tablespoon fresh lemon juice

½ tablespoon dried parsley

½ teaspoon salt

½ teaspoon pepper

Low-fat option: Use light or fat-free mayo

Vegan option: Use vegan mayo

The combination of lemon and garlic in this recipe is extra refreshing! I love to use this aioli on a sandwich or as a spread on vegetable tacos!

What to do:

Add all ingredients to a bowl and mix until fully combined. Mixture should be smooth like a salad dressing. Store in an airtight container in the fridge for 3 to 5 days.

Homemade Tzatziki

Gluten-free | Nut-free
Options: Dairy-free | Low-fat | Vegan

What you'll need:

1 cup yogurt

½ cup grated cucumber

½ teaspoon lemon juice

½ teaspoon olive oil

½ teaspoon garlic

½ teaspoon salt

½ teaspoon pepper

¼ teaspoon dill

Dairy-free option: Use dairy-free yogurt
Low-fat option: Use fat-free yogurt
Vegan option: Use vegan Greek yogurt

This homemade tzatziki is a lifesaver! For years, I had been buying tzatziki and never knew how easy it was to make. Once I made it from scratch, I never bought it again! It's an easy recipe and very refreshing! Plus, it's easy to make vegan or low-fat!

What to do:

Combine all ingredients in a bowl. Mix together. Refrigerate for 1 hour before serving. Store in an airtight container in the fridge for 3 to 5 days.

Grapefruit Mustard Vinaigrette

Yield: ½ cup

Gluten-free | Dairy-free | Nut-free
Options: Low-fat | Low-sugar | Vegan

What you'll need:

3 tablespoons grapefruit juice

2–3 tablespoons olive oil

1 teaspoon sugar-free maple syrup, honey, or agave

2 tablespoons mayonnaise

1 tablespoon Dijon mustard

½ teaspoon garlic

½ teaspoon salt

½ teaspoon pepper

Low-fat option: Use light or fat-free mayo

Low-sugar option: Use sugar-free maple syrup

Vegan option: Use sugar-free maple syrup, vegan honey, or agave and vegan mayo

This grapefruit mustard vinaigrette is the perfect refreshing summer salad dressing. It's perfect for chopped salads and a great healthy option.

What to do:

Combine all ingredients in a bowl. Mix together. Refrigerate for 1 hour before serving. Store in an airtight container in the fridge for 3 to 5 days.

Honey Mustard Vinaigrette

Yield: ½ cup

Gluten-free | Dairy-free | Nut-free
Options: Lower-sugar | Vegan

What you'll need:

1½ tablespoons Dijon mustard

3 tablespoons red wine vinegar

3 tablespoons olive oil

1 tablespoon lemon juice

1 teaspoon maple syrup, honey, or agave

Low-sugar option: Use sugar-free maple syrup

Vegan option: Use sugar-free maple syrup, vegan honey, or agave

I love a good honey mustard, but there's nothing like making your own. You know exactly what healthy ingredients are in it, no preservatives, and it's a clean way to enjoy a salad!

What to do:

Combine all ingredients in a bowl. Mix together. Refrigerate for 1 hour before serving. Store in an airtight container in the fridge for 3 to 5 days.

Chimichurri Herb Vinaigrette

Yield: ¼ cup

Gluten-free | Dairy-free | Nut-free | Vegan

What you'll need:

1 tablespoon red wine vinegar

1 tablespoon olive oil

1 tablespoon balsamic

½ teaspoon oregano

½ teaspoon salt

½ teaspoon pepper

½ teaspoon parsley

½ teaspoon garlic

½ teaspoon red pepper flakes

This recipe is naturally gluten-free, dairy-free, nut-free, and vegan! It's easy to throw together with dried spices you already have in your pantry. No ingredients you can't pronounce and no preservatives!

What to do:

Add all ingredients to a bowl and mix until fully combined. Mixture should be smooth like a salad dressing. Store in an airtight container in the fridge for 3 to 5 days.

Red Pepper Aioli

Yield: ¾ cup

Gluten-free | Dairy-free | Nut-free
Options: Low-fat | Vegan

What you'll need:

1 full roasted red pepper, jarred or home roasted

3 tablespoons diced onions, sautéed until soft and lightly browned

¼ cup mayonnaise

1 tablespoon olive oil

½ teaspoon salt

½ teaspoon pepper

½ teaspoon garlic powder

Low-fat option: Use light or fat-free mayo

Vegan option: Use vegan mayo

This red pepper aioli is the perfect spread for vegetarian tacos. It's smooth, creamy, and full of that roasted red pepper flavor.

What to do:

Add all ingredients to a blender or food processor and blend until fully combined. Aioli should be the same consistency as mayo. If aioli is too thick, add 1 tablespoon more mayo or olive oil and blend again. Store in an airtight container in the fridge for 3 to 5 days.

Campfire Sauce

Yield: ¾ cup

Gluten-free | Dairy-free | Nut-free
Options: Low-fat | Lower-sugar | Vegan

What you'll need:

½ teaspoon garlic powder

⅓ cup BBQ sauce

⅓ cup mayonnaise

½ teaspoon chili powder

½ teaspoon hot sauce

Low-fat option: Use light or fat-free mayo

Lower-sugar option: Use sugar-free BBQ sauce

Vegan option: Use vegan mayo

This campfire sauce is the perfect match for my french fries recipe (page 126), polenta fry recipe (page 127), or gluten-free chicken fingers (page 126)! It's smoky and has a little bit of a kick!

What to do:

Combine all ingredients in a bowl. Mix together and serve. Store in an airtight container in the fridge for 3 to 5 days.

Goldrush Sauce

Yield: ⅔ cup

Gluten-free | Dairy-free | Nut-free
Options: Low-fat | Low-sugar | Vegan

What you'll need:

½ teaspoon garlic powder

⅓ cup BBQ sauce

⅓ cup honey mustard

½ teaspoon hot sauce

Low-fat option: Use light or fat-free honey mustard

Low-sugar option: Use sugar-free BBQ sauce

Vegan option: Use vegan honey mustard

Goldrush sauce is the perfect combo of sweet and smoky. It's a blend of BBQ sauce and honey mustard that's the perfect match for my french fries recipe (page 126), polenta fry recipe (page 127), or gluten-free chicken fingers (page 126)!

What to do:

Combine all ingredients in a bowl. Mix together and serve. Store in an airtight container in the fridge for 3 to 5 days.

Creamy Asian Dressing

Yield: ¾ cup

Gluten-free | Dairy-free | Nut-free
Options: Low-fat | Vegan

What you'll need:

2 tablespoons honey

1½ tablespoons rice wine vinegar

⅓ cup mayonnaise

1 tablespoon lime juice

1 teaspoon Dijon mustard

¼ teaspoon sesame oil

1 teaspoon garlic powder

Low-fat option: Use light or fat-free mayo

Vegan option: Use sugar-free maple syrup, vegan honey, or agave and vegan mayo

This dressing is a healthy play on a salad I used to order when I was younger. It's creamy but has a fun Asian flair. This dressing is perfect on my Asian Chicken Salad (page 91)!

What to do:

Combine all ingredients in a bowl. Mix together. Refrigerate 1 hour before serving. Store in an airtight container in the fridge for 3 to 5 days.

Two-Ingredient Spicy Buffalo Sauce

Yield: 1½ cups

Gluten-free | Dairy-free | Nut-free | Vegan

What you'll need:

½ cup vegan butter

¾–1 cup hot sauce (the more hot sauce, the spicier the buffalo sauce!)

You'll never buy buffalo sauce from the store again after this! This two-ingredient buffalo sauce is made with only hot sauce and vegan butter. Plus, you can make it as spicy or as mild as you want!

What to do:

In a medium-sized saucepan, add both ingredients and cook on medium-low heat for 5 to 10 minutes. Butter will fully melt. Once butter is melted, continue mixing until butter and hot sauce are fully combined. Mixture should be smooth. Remove from the stove and pour in a small bowl for serving or store in an airtight container in the fridge for 3 to 5 days.

Make Your Own Charcuterie Board, page 46

The Food Before the Food

If I were to ask you what your favorite part of a meal is, what would you say? Hands down, it's the appetizers for me. Honestly, whoever invented eating food before the main food really deserves a medal. Whether it be a warm, indulgent goat cheese crostini, or a healthy and light caramelized onion dip, the food before the food is the most important part. The appetizers set up the expectation for the entire meal, so this chapter will help you make sure the appetizers before your meals are absolutely drool-worthy!

Antipasto on a Stick

Yield: 25 skewers

Gluten-free | Nut-free
Options: Dairy-free | Low-fat | Vegan

What you'll need:

25 mini wooden skewers

¼ pound sliced salami

¼ pound sliced pepperoni or turkey pepperoni

¼ pound provolone

¼ pound prosciutto

1 cup mozzarella

1 orange

Dairy-free option: Use any dairy-free cheeses

Low-fat option: Use turkey pepperoni instead of standard pepperoni. Feel free to sub out other meats for leaner options, such as low-sodium ham instead of prosciutto, etc. Swap low-fat cheeses.

Vegan option: Use any meatless/vegan meats and vegan/dairy-free cheeses

Every year for Easter, my family makes an Italian antipasto with a recipe that was passed down from my great-grandparents to my grandparents down to my parents. My grandparents still make it; all of my aunts and uncles and cousins make it, and we each put our own spin on it! My spin is to make it handheld! I use the same ingredients my dad used, and his dad used, but I put it on a skewer!

What you'll do:

On a cutting board, cut all the cheese into 1-inch cubes. Slice up orange wedges into 1-inch pieces. Layer the meats, cheese, and oranges on the stick. Holding the mini skewer in one hand, slide the cheese cubes, meats, and oranges up the skewer until the skewer is full. You don't want it to be packed with as much food as possible. Each item should be slightly spaced apart, leaving more room on the top and bottom ends for holding. I like to keep the cheese and oranges for the ends to make sure nothing falls off. The meats, I try to handle as little as possible so they don't look overworked. I just fold them into halves or quarters and slide them onto the stick.

Feel free to make this your own by adding more fruits or vegetables, such as tomatoes, grapes, blueberries, or strawberries.

(Continued on next page)

Five More Combinations
to Make These Skewers Your Own

Skewer appetizers are my favorite to bring to a party or get-together because you can mix and match with so many different ingredients that you'll be bringing a new recipe every time. From caprese skewers with mozzarella and tomatoes to pasta salad skewers with gluten-free tortellini and tomatoes, the combinations are endless.

Greek Skewers
Cherry tomatoes + marinated olives + cucumbers + mozzarella/vegan mozzarella + olive oil drizzle + salt + pepper

Caprese Skewers
Cherry tomatoes + mozzarella/vegan mozzarella + basil + olive oil drizzle + balsamic glaze + salt + pepper

Pear + Brie Cheese Skewers
Pears cut into 1-inch cubes + brie cheese + candied pecans + arugula + olive oil drizzle + balsamic glaze

Pasta Salad Skewers
Fully cooked gluten free tortellini + cherry tomatoes + mozzarella/vegan mozzarella + basil + olive oil drizzle + garlic salt + pepper + oregano

Beets + Feta
Roasted beets cut into 1-inch cubes + feta cheese/vegan feta cheese + arugula + candied pecans + honey drizzle

Air Fryer Sausage and Pepper Skewers

Yield: 25 skewers

Gluten-free | Dairy-free | Nut-free
Option: Vegan/vegetarian

What you'll need:

6 precooked chicken sausages

2–3 bell peppers

1 zucchini

1 teaspoon salt

1 teaspoon pepper

2 teaspoon sesame seeds

Vegan/vegetarian: Use vegan sausage!

This sausage and pepper recipe is a healthier play on traditional sausage and peppers but on a skewer! It uses chicken sausage instead of pork sausage for a leaner option. Since the skewers are air-fried, they are made without butter or oil and make for an easy handheld appetizer in only 15 minutes!

What to do:

Add 2 to 3 cups of water to a 9 × 12–inch baking dish. Add the wooden skewers to the dish and soak for 30 minutes to 1 hour to prevent burning.

On a large cutting board, cut each precooked sausage into 1-inch round slices. Next, cut the peppers and zucchini into similar-sized pieces so they cook evenly.

Slide the pepper slices, zucchini slices, and sausages onto the skewers, alternating as you go: pepper, zucchini, sausage, pepper, zucchini, sausage, etc. Once complete, spray the skewers with light cooking spray and season with salt, pepper, and sesame seeds.

Place the skewers into a preheated air fryer on 390°F and cook for 9 to 14 minutes until sausage is fully cooked and both sausage and vegetables are lightly charred.

Simple and Healthy Caramelized Onion Dip

Yield: 2 cups

Gluten-free | Nut-free | Vegetarian
Options: Dairy-free | Low-fat | Vegan

What you'll need:

3 sweet onions

1 tablespoon olive oil for caramelizing onions

2 cups fat-free Greek yogurt or vegan yogurt

1 teaspoon garlic salt

1 teaspoon pepper

Dairy-free option: Use dairy-free/vegan yogurt

Low-fat option: Use fat-free yogurt

Vegan option: Use vegan yogurt

The easiest caramelized onion dip you'll ever make. It's gluten-free, low-fat, and ready in 15 minutes! It's perfect for a quick appetizer or party snack. It has minimal clean up and is actually secretly healthy!

What to do:

On a cutting board, slice onions into thin ¼-inch strips. The thinner the better! Add onions to a frying pan with olive oil and slow cook on medium-low heat until onions are caramelized and brown. Make sure to slow roast so they don't burn.

In a separate bowl, place Greek yogurt, salt, and pepper in a bowl. Add caramelized onions. Mix together and chill for 1 hour before serving. Serve with potato chips, fresh vegetables, or crackers!

BBQ Chicken Dip

Yield: 10 servings

Gluten-free | Nut-free
Options: Dairy-free | Lower-fat | Lower-sugar | Vegan | Vegetarian

What you'll need:

1 red bell pepper

1 small red onion

½ tablespoon olive oil

2 cups shredded chicken or jackfruit

2 cups BBQ sauce, divided

1 cup ranch, divided

1 cup cream cheese

2 cups cheddar cheese, shredded and divided

2 tablespoons chopped chives, for topping

Dairy-free option: Use vegan/dairy-free cheese, vegan/dairy-free ranch, and vegan/dairy-free cream cheese

Lower-fat option: Use fat-free cheese, low-fat cream cheese, and fat-free ranch

Lower-sugar option: Use sugar-free BBQ sauce

Vegan option: Use shredded jackfruit, vegan/dairy-free cheese, vegan/dairy-free ranch, and vegan/dairy-free cream cheese

Vegetarian option: Use shredded jackfruit

To put it lightly, my friends and I are obsessed with this BBQ chicken dip. Ever since college, whenever we all get together, someone would bring this dip. A weekend at the beach? BBQ chicken dip. Dinner and drinks at someone's apartment? BBQ chicken dip. Getting together to celebrate a birthday, engagement, or pregnancy? BBQ chicken dip. So, to say you'll be making this dip for every party or get together for the foreseeable future is an understatement.

What to do:

Preheat oven to 350°F. On a cutting board, slice the pepper and onion into ¼-inch-thick slices. Add to a frying pan with olive oil and cook on medium-low heat for 10 to 15 minutes until peppers and onions are soft and browned.

Move cooked peppers and onions to a medium-sized bowl. Add in shredded chicken or jackfruit. Next add 1½ cups of BBQ sauce and ½ cup of ranch. Mix in cream cheese. Add 1 cup cheddar cheese. Make sure all ingredients are fully combined.

Pour into a 9 × 9–inch baking dish. Cover with remaining cheddar cheese. Bake, covered, for 20 to 30 minutes until dip is fully warmed. Remove from oven. Drizzle with remaining BBQ sauce and ranch. Top with chopped chives.

Serve with corn tortilla chips, gluten-free chips, gluten-free pretzels, or fresh vegetables for dipping.

(Continued on next page)

Want to make this into nachos? Cut the recipe in half. Line a baking sheet with corn tortilla chips. Top the chips with BBQ chicken dip and extra cheddar cheese.

Want to make these into taquitos? Warm corn tortillas in the oven or microwave for a few minutes. Corn tortillas are easier to roll when warmed. Add 2 heaping scoops to a corn tortilla. Roll up and air-fry for 5 to 10 minutes until crispy. Serve with ranch dipping sauce!

Want to make this into a taco chicken dip? Sub taco sauce for BBQ sauce. Fold in corn and black beans before baking. Top with diced chives.

Want to make this a buffalo chicken dip? Sub Two-Ingredient Spicy Buffalo Sauce (page 33) for BBQ sauce! Top with fat-free feta and diced tomatoes.

Everything-but-the-Bread Italian Hoagie Dip

Yield: 10 servings

Gluten-free | Nut-free
Options: Dairy-free | Low-fat

What you'll need:

¼ pound slices provolone, diced

¼ pound turkey cold cut, diced

¼ pound pepperoni ori turkey pepperoni, diced

½ cup butter lettuce or romaine lettuce, shredded

½ cup of banana peppers, diced

½ cup of roasted red peppers, diced

¼ cup red onion, diced

2-3 tablespoons red wine vinegar

2-3 tablespoons balsamic vinaigrette

½ cup low fat or fat free mayo

½ tablespoon dried oregano

½ tablespoon garlic

salt and pepper, to taste

Dairy-free option: Use vegan/dairy-free cheese for dairy-free recipe

Low-fat option: Use fat-free or low-fat cheese

Some people say hero, some people say sub, and some people say hoagie. I'm not here to decide which name is correct, but I am here to say that no matter what you call it, if you love the sandwich, you'll love this dip.

What to do:

Chop all ingredients as small as you can! The smaller the better to create the perfect bite. Add all chopped ingredients to a bowl. Mix together. Chill for 2 hours before serving.

Serve with corn tortilla chips, gluten-free chips, gluten-free pretzels, or fresh vegetables for dipping.

Cranberry and Goat Cheese Crostinis

Yield: 15–20 crostinis

Gluten-free | Nut-free
Options: Dairy-free | Lower-fat | Vegan | Vegetarian

What you'll need:

1 gluten-free baguette

4 ounces goat cheese

¼ cup cranberry jam

1 dried turkey stick, or 3 slices of prosciutto, or any other cured meat

1 tablespoon olive oil

1 teaspoon salt

1 teaspoon pepper

1 tablespoon green onions, chopped

Dairy-free option: Use vegan/dairy-free goat cheese or vegan/dairy-free cream cheese

Lower-fat option: Use fat-free or low-fat cream cheese instead of goat cheese

Vegan option: Skip the prosciutto or use vegan meat. Use vegan goat cheese or vegan cream cheese.

Vegetarian option: Skip the meat or use vegan meat

You're going to want to save these crostinis! I made these appetizers using goat cheese, cranberry jam, and green onions, and they're 100% a crowd pleaser! They're gluten-free, full of flavor, and who can say no to a bite-sized treat!?

What to do:

Preheat oven to 350°F. Slice the baguette into 1-inch-thick slices. Add slices to a lined baking sheet, and bake for approximately 6 to 8 minutes until crispy and browned. Remove crostinis. Spread the goat cheese on each of the crostini slices. Top with cranberry jam and prosciutto. Drizzle with olive oil. Top with salt, pepper, and chopped green onions. Serve and enjoy!

Make Your Own Charcuterie Board

Makes 1 board

Gluten-free | Nut-free
Options: Dairy-free | Low-carb | Low-fat | Vegan | Vegetarian

I am a huge fan of charcuterie boards! These boards are a really easy way to have a little something for everyone. I like to include vegan options, such as vegan cheeses or fruit. I include dairy-free options, such as meats and gluten-free pretzels. I like to make sure there's fresh fruit available for anyone watching their sugar intake or fat intake. You can really put anything on the charcuterie board, but I like to break up my boards into a meat section, a cheese section, and a crunchy snack section. Then, I always add fresh greens, usually rosemary, to give it a pop of color.

Dairy-free option: Use vegan/dairy-free cheeses

Low-carb option: Serve with cauliflower crackers and fruit

Low-fat option: Serve with lean meats and fat-free cheese options

Vegan option: Skip the meats altogether or use vegan meat and use vegan/dairy-free cheese

Vegetarian option: Skip the meats altogether or use vegan meat

For your meat section:
For the meats, I recommend choosing from 2 to 3 different textured meats.

Choose 1 to 2 hard sausages and cut thick slices. I always add prosciutto to mine; it's thin and soft and easy to add to a cracker. Pepperoni is always a good option, or turkey pepperonis. Turkey pepperoni slices are usually smaller and leaner for a good healthy option.

Some more ideas include: salami, sopressata, chorizo.

For your cheese section:
Any kind of dairy or vegan cheese will work! I like to choose 2 to 3 cheeses that you can pick up by hand; they're soft and you won't need a cracker for them. Then usually 1 to 2 soft cheeses or even a dip for crackers. Try for different textured cheese options on your board.

Some hard cheeses include: cheddar, asiago, parmesan, Manchego, Gruyère, gouda.

Some soft cheeses include: goat cheese, burrata, mozzarella, brie.

For your crunchy snack section:
Try any of these: gluten-free crackers, gluten-free pretzels, any kind of crunchy snack foods or chips, crunchy corn, or crunchy chickpeas.

Four-Ingredient Banana Waffles, page 63

Breakfasts on the Sweeter Side

Waking up to the smell of bacon and a warm breakfast is a dreamy start to my day. And if I could start every single day that way, trust me, I would. Sweet breakfasts are really an excuse to have dessert in the morning, in my opinion. I feel very strongly about loading up my waffles with chocolate chips, my French toast with fruit, and sprinkling some powdered sugar on top. A big breakfast is the best way to start the day. Whether it be gluten-free French toast with sugar-free syrup, banana waffles, or mini pancake loaves, you're going to want to wake up to these breakfast options.

Pumpkin Pie French Toast

Yield: 1 breakfast

Gluten-free | Nut-free
Options: Dairy-free | Low-fat | Vegan

For your toast:

2 eggs or ⅓ cup egg whites

⅓ cup pumpkin purée

2 tablespoons plant-based milk

2 tablespoons cinnamon or pumpkin pie spice

1 tablespoon vegan butter or light oil spray

3 slices of gluten-free bread or bread of choice

For your toppings:

All the syrup you want! I used sugar-free!

All the berries you want! I prefer fresh
strawberries and blueberries.

Any extra breakfast goodies! I like to add
turkey bacon, regular bacon, or sautéed
breakfast potatoes.

Dairy-free option: Use plant-based milk
and vegan butter. Make sure your bread
is dairy-free, as well.

Low-fat option: Use egg whites.

Vegan option: Use (1) mashed banana
instead of eggs, plant-based milk, and
vegan butter. Make sure your bread is
vegan.

There's nothing cozier than a good pumpkin recipe. Whether it be pumpkin bread, pumpkin pie, or pumpkin French toast—count me in. This pumpkin pie French toast is the perfect start to a crisp fall day. I love topping mine with maple syrup, fresh berries, and extra cinnamon!

What to do:

Combine eggs, pumpkin purée, plant-based milk, and cinnamon/pumpkin pie spice in a shallow dish. Mix until fully blended.

Melt butter or spray oil in a large frying pan over medium heat.

Dip one piece of bread into the mixture, covering both sides. Then add to the pan. I put 4 pieces in the pan at once! You can do however many fit.

Cook both sides for 2 to 4 minutes until the edges become crispy. Repeat until all the French toast is made!

Chocolate Peanut Butter French Toast Sticks

Yield: 1 breakfast

Gluten-free
Options: Dairy-free | Lower-fat | Lower-sugar | Vegan

What you'll need:

3 slices of gluten-free bread or bread of choice

2 eggs or ⅓ cup egg whites

¼ cup plant-based milk

1 tablespoon cocoa powder

1 tablespoon peanut butter powder

1 tablespoon of sugar, coconut sugar, or sugar substitute

1 tablespoon butter or light oil spray

Dairy-free option: Use plant-based milk and vegan butter. Make sure your bread is dairy-free.

Lower-fat option: Use egg whites or (1) mashed banana for egg

Lower-sugar option: Use sugar substitute

Vegan option: Use (1) mashed banana instead of eggs, plant-based milk, and vegan butter. Make sure your bread is vegan.

There is no better combination than peanut butter and chocolate. Every year, when Easter comes around, I love those chocolate-covered peanut butter eggs. This easy French toast stick recipe is filled with that peanut butter and chocolate flavoring while still being healthy and lower in fat. This recipe uses peanut butter powder to eliminate the unnecessary oil in regular peanut butter. It also uses cocoa powder instead of chocolate to cut back on saturated fats in standard melted chocolate chips. You have the option to use egg whites instead of full eggs and plant-based milk instead of full-fat dairy milk. Now you can enjoy a guilt-free chocolate and peanut butter recipe every day of the week!

What to do:

Evenly slice gluten-free bread into 1-inch strips. Set aside.

In a bowl, combine eggs and milk. Mix thoroughly. Add cocoa powder, peanut butter powder, and sugar. Mix again.

Dip each strip into a wet mixture. Make sure each piece is evenly coated.

Spray or add vegan butter to a frying pan on medium heat. Once pan is evenly coated, add French toast sticks.

Cook for approximately 3 minutes, until crispy, and then flip over and cook on the opposite side for 3 additional minutes.

Remove French toast sticks to a serving plate. Serve with sugar-free maple syrup, if desired.

Cinnamon Bun French Toast

Yield: 1 breakfast

Gluten-free | Dairy-free | Nut-free
Option: Lower sugar | Vegan

What you'll need:

1 mashed banana

¼ cup plant-based milk

2 tablespoons cinnamon, divided

3 slices gluten-free bread or bread of choice

1 tablespoon vegan butter or light oil spray

Lower-sugar option: Use unsweetened plant milk

Vegan option: Use vegan bread

The smell of warm maple syrup is so nostalgic. It reminds me of waking up on Christmas morning to the smell of a warm breakfast baking. We always have cinnamon buns on Christmas morning, so I wanted to translate that nostalgic cinnamon flavor into a healthy, light, everyday vegan breakfast.

What to do:

In a bowl, fully mash banana until there are no lumps and the consistency resembles applesauce. The mixture should be mushy and smooth. Add plant-based milk and fully combine. Add half the amount of cinnamon to the banana mixture and mix. Dip each slice of bread into liquid mixture evenly, flipping over and coating each side.

Spray or add vegan butter to a frying pan on medium heat. Once pan is evenly coated, add banana-dipped bread. Sprinkle remaining cinnamon on exposed sides while in the pan.

Cook for approximately 3 minutes on each side. When you flip over the slices, the bread should be browned and crispy along the edges and soft in the center. If the bread is not browned, you have flipped too early and will need more time. Once both sides are browned and crisp, remove from the frying pan and plate.

Serve with sugar-free maple syrup, if desired.

Five-Ingredient Churro French Toast

Yield: 1 breakfast

Gluten-free | Dairy-free | Nut-free
Options: Low-fat | Lower-sugar | Vegan

What you'll need:

2 eggs or ⅓ cup egg whites

¼ cup plant-based milk

4 tablespoons sugar, coconut sugar, or sugar
substitute

4 tablespoons cinnamon

3 slices gluten-free bread or bread of choice

1 tablespoon vegan butter or light oil spray

Low-fat option: Use egg whites or (1)
mashed banana

Lower-sugar option: Use sugar substitute

Vegan option: Use (1) mashed banana
in place of egg, plant-based milk, and
vegan butter. Make sure your bread is
vegan.

I have yet to find a gluten-free churro on any menu, and the thought of never having a churro again is devastating. This French toast is lightly pan-fried with vegan butter and coated in cinnamon and sugar in a very churro kind of way! It's fun to serve with warm maple syrup for dipping.

What to do:

Combine eggs (or banana) and plant-based milk in one bowl. Set aside.

Combine the cinnamon and sugar in a separate shallow dish.

Dip each slice of bread into liquid mixture, evenly coating each side.

Spray oil or add vegan butter to a frying pan on medium heat. Once pan is evenly coated, add dipped bread.

Cook for approximately 3 minutes, until crispy, and then flip over and cook on the opposite side for 3 additional minutes.

Remove French toast and immediately add to a separate dish with cinnamon and sugar. Cover each side with the cinnamon and sugar mixture until bread resembles that of a churro. Remove and set onto a serving plate.

Serve with warm, sugar-free maple syrup for dipping. Feel free to make this your own by topping with fresh, warm strawberries, warm blueberries, or slices of bananas baked with sugar. You may also choose to serve with turkey bacon or vegan bacon as a healthy option.

Double Chocolate French Toast

Yield: 1 breakfast

Gluten-free | Dairy-free | Nut-free
Options: Lower-sugar | Vegan

What you'll need:

1 mashed banana

¼ cup plant-based milk

2 tablespoons cocoa powder

2 tablespoons sugar

3 slices gluten-free bread or bread of choice

1 tablespoon vegan butter or light oil spray

2 tablespoons chocolate chips, for topping

2 tablespoons chocolate syrup, for topping

2 tablespoons maple syrup, for topping

Lower-sugar option: Use sugar replacement, unsweetened plant milk, sugar-free chocolate chips, and sugar-free maple syrup

Vegan option: Use coconut sugar, vegan chocolate chips, vegan chocolate syrup, and make sure your bread is vegan

Every Sunday when I was a kid, my family and I used to visit my great-aunt in Hoboken, New Jersey, for Sunday lunch. We'd be presented with a full spread of cold cuts and breads and we'd always end the lunch with pound cake. The chocolate pound cake was my favorite.

What to do:

Combine mashed banana and plant-based milk in one bowl. Add cocoa powder and sugar. Mix and set aside.

Dip each slice of bread into liquid mixture evenly, flipping over and coating each side.

Spray or add vegan butter to a frying pan on medium heat. Once pan is coated evenly, add dipped bread.

Cook for approximately 3 minutes on each side. When you flip over, make sure to add cinnamon to the newly exposed side. When you flip, slices should be browned and crispy. If the bread is not browned, you have flipped too early and the French toast will need more time.

Once both sides are browned and crisp, remove from the pan and plate.

Top with chocolate chips immediately so they melt. Serve with maple and/or chocolate syrup of choice.

Mini Blueberry Pancake Breads

Yield: 8 mini loaves

Gluten-free | Dairy-free | Nut-free
Options: Lower-sugar | Vegan

What you'll need:

2 cups gluten-free pancake mix˙

⅔ cup plant-based milk

1–2 mashed bananas

2 eggs

¼ cup blueberries

˙This mix should not be a "just-add-water" mix.

Lower-sugar option: Use sugar-free pancake mix

Vegan option: Use an egg substitute

Pancakes were one of the first things I learned to make as a kid, so they'll always have a special place in my heart. I love letting them get a little too crisp and topping them with blueberries and extra butter. These mini loaves are made with pancake mix instead of flour, which make them fluffy and essentially a handheld pancake. They make for the perfect breakfast or an even better healthy dessert.

What to do:

Combine ingredients in a bowl. Mix together thoroughly. Add to mini loaf pan. Fill each mini loaf cavity ½ to ¾ full. I have a 15 × 9–inch loaf pan that makes 8 mini loafs.

Bake at 350°F for 25 to 30 minutes until center is set. Remove from oven. Let cool for 15 minutes before serving. Serve with warm blueberries and warm sugar-free maple syrup.

Four-Ingredient Banana Waffles

Yield: 2 waffles

Gluten-free | Dairy-free | Nut-free
Option: Low-fat

What you'll need:

2 bananas (1 cup mashed)

4 eggs

¼ teaspoon baking powder

¼ cup gluten-free flour

Low-fat option: Use (½ cup) egg whites instead of full eggs

For me, the easier the recipe, the more likely I am to make it again and again. This recipe is as easy as it gets! You only need bananas, eggs, baking powder, and gluten-free flour. Choose from any toppings you want! I love serving these waffles with turkey bacon, vegan chocolate chips, and fresh berries.

What to do

Preheat the waffle iron to medium-high temperature. In a medium-sized bowl, mash the bananas. Then mix in the eggs, baking powder, and gluten-free flour.

Spray the waffle iron with light cooking spray if the iron is not nonstick. Add half the batter. Cook for 3 to 5 minutes until waffle is crispy around the edges and fluffy in the center. Cook time may vary for each waffle iron.

Remove from iron and cook remaining half of batter to make the second waffle. Top with sugar-free syrup, berries, or vegan chocolate chips, and enjoy!

Savory Breakfasts

I'm a huge fan of starting the day off with some healthy avocado toast and a warm cup of green tea. Whether you're starting the morning off running out the door and need a quick breakfast on the go, or have some extra time to sit down and savor each bite, these recipes will keep you feeling full and healthy all day long. This savory breakfast chapter features filling recipes with full eggs and healthy proteins, as well as breakfasts on the lighter side with egg whites and spinach.

Avocado Toast with Scrambled Eggs, Fat-Free Feta, Salsa, and Chives, page 67

Mix-and-Match
Avocado Toasts

If avocado toast is on the menu at a restaurant (and if they have gluten-free bread), I will always order it. There's so many ways to make avocado toast: sliced, mashed, or cubed, or paired with vegetables, different oils, or toppings. It's packed with healthy nutrients, healthy fats, and if you're making avocado toast at home, it takes fewer than 10 minutes.

Step 1. Select your toast.

Use any toast you want for this breakfast or snack! Gluten-free bread, vegan bread, fresh homemade bread, gluten-free English muffins, gluten-free Italian bread, gluten-free baguettes, gluten-free bagels, etc. I prefer a crispy, toasted option that's slightly warm from the toaster or oven.

Step 2. Prepare your avocado.

For 1 slice of avocado toast, you will need approximately ¼ of an avocado. For 2 slices of avocado toast, you will need ½ an avocado. To slice thinly, hold the avocado in your hand and slice down the center longways. Twist to separate, and select the half without the pit. Wrap up the half with the pit and add back to the refrigerator. Peel one corner off by pulling the skin back easily in one motion. If the avocado is ripe, the skin will come right off. Slice into thin slices. Add to your toast.

Store the unused half in a plastic ziptop bag or rolled in plastic wrap. Make sure to get out as much air as you can so the avocado doesn't brown.

If the avocado does not separate easily, or the skin doesn't peel off easily, don't stress. You can always scoop out the avocado with a spoon and mash.

How do you know when an avocado is ripe?

An easy way to tell if an avocado is ripe is by removing the cap or hat at the top. If the area under the cap is green or yellow, then the avocado is ripe and ready to use. If the area under the cap is brown, the avocado has passed its ripe stage and could be brown inside.

Another way to tell if an avocado is ripe is by how hard or soft the avocado feels when gently squeezing in your hand. If the avocado is very hard, like a baseball, it is not ripe and needs a few more days. If the avocado is slightly soft and you can feel the give with little effort, that means the avocado is likely ripe. If the avocado is very soft and you are easily able to squeeze, the softness could mean the avocado is too ripe and past its prime (you will likely not want to use it). You can set the avocado in the freezer to use in a baking recipe as a substitute for oil for a 1:1 ratio.

How to keep your avocados ripe?
As soon as the avocado starts to feel soft to the touch, pop the avocado into the refrigerator until you are ready to use. This works best if the avocado is not sliced yet. The cool air stunts the growth of the avocado and will preserve the ripeness. The avocado will not continue to ripen in the refrigerator. You can leave the avocado in the fridge for 1 to 3 days.

Step 3: Select your topping combinations.
Choose from any of the combinations below or mix and match to create your own!

15 Combinations to Make This Avocado Toast Your Own

1. Arugula Pesto Aioli (page 25) + fried egg + arugula
2. Lemon Garlic Aioli (page 26) + arugula + parmesan cheese or vegan parmesan cheese + olive oil drizzle + garlic salt + pepper
3. Homemade Tzatziki (page 27) + sliced tomatoes + sliced cucumbers + arugula
4. Red Pepper Aioli (page 30) + roasted red pepper slices + arugula + olive oil drizzle + salt + pepper
5. Crispy crumbled turkey bacon + caramelized onions + goat cheese or fat-free feta or vegan feta
6. 1 poached egg + vegan/dairy-free cream cheese + salt + pepper + red pepper flakes
7. 1 fried egg + red pepper flakes + salt + pepper + olive oil drizzle + dairy-free parmesan
8. 1 hard-boiled egg sliced into thin slices + salt + pepper + sriracha
9. 1 poached egg + salt + pepper + olive oil drizzle
10. Tomato slices + fat-free or vegan feta + pumpkin seeds + olive oil drizzle
11. Goat cheese or fat-free feta or vegan feta + salted tomato slices + balsamic glaze
12. Diced tomatoes + salt + pepper + olive oil drizzle + regular or hot honey
13. Tomato slices + mozzarella slices + salt + pepper + red pepper flakes + balsamic glaze
14. Scrambled eggs, egg whites, or scrambled tofu "eggs" + salsa
15. Scrambled eggs, egg whites, or scrambled tofu "eggs" + fat-free or vegan feta + oven-roasted tomatoes + diced red onion

Healthy Spinach and Egg White Casserole

Yield: 6 slices

Gluten-free | Low-carb | Nut-free | Vegetarian
Options: Dairy-free | Low-fat

What you'll need:

6 gluten-free cauliflower hash browns

1⅔ cup liquid egg whites

⅔ cup plant-based milk

2 cups fresh spinach

¼ cup fat-free feta or vegan/dairy-free feta

2 tablespoons diced red onion

1 teaspoon salt

1 teaspoon pepper

1 tablespoon garlic powder

Dairy-free option: Use plant-based milk and vegan/dairy-free feta

Low-fat option: Use fat-free feta

How to Meal Prep This

You can bake this on Sunday mornings and divide the casserole into 6 slices for a healthy breakfast meal prep. Add each slice to an airtight Tupperware and store in the fridge for the week. It's easy to heat up before a busy day or perfect to bring with you to work! Microwave each slice for approximately 60 seconds or until it's warm!

This healthy spinach and feta egg white casserole is made completely with egg whites and no full eggs, which means it is low in saturated fat. There is also no oil or butter. I like to top each warm slice with Homemade Tzatziki (page 27), a drizzle of Red Pepper Aioli (page 30), and some extra feta. To add more protein, mix in breakfast chicken sausage, breakfast turkey sausage, or turkey bacon crumbles.

What to do:

Preheat the oven to 400°F.

Line a 9 × 9–inch dish with parchment paper or spray with light oil spray to keep the casserole from sticking.

Once hash browns are thawed, crumble the cauliflower hash browns and cover the bottom of a 9 × 9–inch baking dish. Press down to create an even layer.

In a separate bowl, combine egg whites and plant-based milk. Add the spinach, feta, raw onion, salt, pepper, and garlic powder to the egg mixture. Mix thoroughly and then pour over cauliflower hash browns.

Cover with aluminum foil and bake for 30 to 40 minutes or until the center is set. Remove from the oven and cut into 6 slices.

Serve with a dollop of Homemade Tzatziki (page 27), a drizzle of Red Pepper Aioli (page 30), and extra feta.

Loaded Mashed Potato Waffles

Yield: 2–3 waffles

Gluten-free | Nut-free
Options: Dairy-free | Low-fat | Vegan

What you'll need:

2 cups mashed potatoes

¼ cup egg whites

¼ cup plant-based milk

¼ cup shredded cheddar

¼ cup brown-rice flour or gluten-free flour blend

1 teaspoon baking powder

1 tablespoon garlic

2 teaspoons parsley

light oil spray

Dairy-free option: Use vegan cheese and plant-based milk

Low-fat option: Use egg whites and fat-free cheese

Vegan option: Use vegan cheese, plant-based milk, and an egg substitute

These mashed potato waffles are perfect when you have left over mashed potatoes sitting around in the fridge. Feel free to use any kind of mashed potato leftovers you have, even if they have salt + pepper, butter, cheese, chives, etc. already in them. It's perfect for those holiday leftovers, too. These loaded mashed potato waffles are the healthy breakfast version of potato skins.

What to do:

Preheat waffle iron to medium-high setting.

Combine all ingredients except spray into a bowl and mix to create a thick batter. If the potatoes are too wet or moist, add some extra rice flour to thicken the mixture and dry out the consistency. This may happen if your leftovers had too much butter or milk in them.

Spray waffle iron with light oil spray and pour batter into waffle iron. Close waffle iron and cook for 4 to 6 minutes until the waffle is crispy! Repeat until all batter is used.

If desired, top with a chives, fried egg, scrambled eggs, or turkey bacon!

Potato and Egg Breakfast Tacos

Yield: 3 tacos

Gluten-free | Dairy-free | Nut-free
Options: Low-fat | Vegan

What you'll need:

1 small white potato

1 tablespoon garlic

1 teaspoon salt

1 teaspoon pepper

light oil spray

¼ cup egg whites + 2 eggs

½ cup fresh spinach

3 corn tortillas

3 slices bacon

¼ cup diced tomatoes

½ cup salsa

Low-fat option: Use low-sodium or turkey bacon and tofu scramble option (page 74)

Vegan option: Use egg substitutes or scrambled tofu (page 74). Use vegan bacon.

If you're the type of person who likes tacos, and likes breakfast, and has a hard time choosing which is better, this recipe is for you! I love a good breakfast . . . but small, warm corn tortillas are hard to pass up, as well. These breakfast tacos won't make you choose between the two. These tacos are packed with all your favorite breakfast flavors on top of a warm corn tortilla topped with fresh greens.

What to do:

Preheat the oven to 350°F.

Make the potatoes

Slice the small white potato into ½-inch cubes. Add to bowl and toss with garlic, salt, and pepper. Spray lightly with light oil spray, if needed to get the seasoning to stick. Add the potatoes to the air fryer and cook on 390°F for 8 to 12 minutes until potatoes are crispy. Add extra 2 to 3 minutes for larger cubes or for extra crispiness.

Make the eggs

In a small bowl, while potatoes are cooking, combine the egg whites and eggs. Beat together until fully combined. In a frying pan on medium heat, add the fresh spinach and lightly spray with light oil spray. After approximately 3 minutes, the spinach should be fully cooked and wilted. Next, add the egg mixture, slowly coating the entire bottom of the frying pan. After 1 to 2 minutes, once eggs have started cooking, use a spatula to pull the edges in to create folds of eggs. Let any excess liquid fall to the outside edges to finish cooking.

(Continued on page 74)

Warm the corn tortillas
Add corn tortillas to the preheated oven and warm for 2 to 4 minutes so the tortillas are warm and easier to work with.

Make the bacon
Make the bacon in the air fryer, microwave, or oven. I like mine very dark and crispy. It's easier to crumble that way!

Set it up
Remove corn tortillas and set onto a serving plate. Divide the eggs into 3 equal sections. Add cooked eggs with spinach on top of each tortilla. Top with crispy potatoes, salsa, diced tomatoes, and crumbled bacon.

Healthy Hack!

This recipe uses a combination of eggs and egg whites together as a healthy hack to cut back on saturated fat and cholesterol.

- Use turkey bacon instead of regular bacon to reduce the amount of saturated fat, calories, sodium, and nitrates. You can also use low-sodium bacon.
- This recipe uses no cheese to ensure the breakfast tacos are naturally dairy free and low in saturated fat. You also have the option to add fat-free, vegan, or dairy-free cheese if you choose to.
- Cook your crispy breakfast potatoes in an air fryer to ensure you are not using too much oil as you would in a pan.

Tofu Scramble

In a pan, add tofu, turmeric, paprika, Dijon mustard, garlic powder, onion powder, salt, and pepper. Season to your preference. On medium heat, scramble all ingredients together to mimic eggs. Cook for 5 to 7 minutes.

Low-Carb Taco Breakfast Casserole

Yield: 6 slices

Gluten-free | Dairy-free | Low-carb | Nut-free | Vegetarian
Option: Low-fat

What you'll need:

6 gluten-free cauliflower hash browns

2 tablespoons low-sodium taco seasoning

5 eggs

⅔ cup liquid egg whites

⅔ cup plant-based milk

½ cup diced peppers

¼ cup diced white onion

salsa

Vegan Avocado Crema (page 24)

Low-fat option: Eliminate the eggs and double the egg whites

This breakfast casserole makes for the perfect healthy start to the day! This recipe is low carb because it uses cauliflower hash browns but is still filling since there's both egg whites and whole eggs. I love mixing eggs and egg whites together to give you the feeling of the meal being heartier while still being healthy. Of course, feel free to use all whole eggs or all egg whites, but combining them makes me feel like I'm eating more, without the added saturated fat of more egg yolks. Want to make this even healthier? Add more vegetables!

What to do:

Thaw the hash browns in a bowl on the counter for 30 minutes. Preheat the oven to 400°F.

Line a 9 × 9–inch dish with parchment paper or spray with light oil spray to keep the casserole from sticking. Once hash browns are thawed, crumble them and cover the bottom of the baking dish. Press down to create an even layer.

Top hash-brown layer evenly with taco seasoning.

In a separate bowl, combine eggs, egg whites, and plant-based milk. Mix thoroughly and then pour over cauliflower hash browns. Top with diced peppers and onions.

Cover with aluminum foil and bake for 30 to 40 minutes or until the center is set. Remove from the oven and cut into 6 slices.

Serve with salsa and top with Vegan Avocado Crema.

(Continued on page 77)

Low-Carb Taco Breakfast Casserole, page 75

Save Some Time

To partially prepare this casserole ahead of time, sauté the peppers and onions in a frying pan and store in an airtight container for 2 to 3 days in the fridge. When you are ready to make the casserole, just add your precooked vegetables and you won't have to worry about cooking the casserole longer to make sure the vegetables are soft.

A Note on Cauliflower Hash Browns

Use any kind of vegetable or potato hash browns for this dish. The cauliflower hash brown makes this recipe low carb. If you do not have any hash browns, use any kind of potato tater tot or vegetable tater tot. Just line the bottom of the baking dish with the tots and continue with the recipe per the directions.

Feel free to make this casserole your own by adding any extra topping you'd normally add to your tacos. You can add black beans, refried beans, red onion, turkey bacon crumbles, etc. at the end when you add your peppers. Make sure the extra toppings are evenly distributed across the casserole.

The Ultimate Caesar Salad with air-fried tater tots instead of Herbed Croutons, page 97

Loaded (Non-Boring!) Salads

I love a good salad, especially when it's heavy on the toppings. I like a 1:1 ratio for greens to toppings. I love to load up salads with vegetables and healthy grains so I'm full throughout the day. No one wants to eat a boring bowl of leafy greens.

A Quick Note on My Salads

All the salads in this chapter are choose-your-own-adventure style. Each recipe will have a base of greens, toppings, a variety of cheese to choose from, grains, and healthy proteins.

Salad Base:
For the green salad base, you'll be able to choose from arugula, butter lettuce, romaine, green leaf lettuce, or any other leafy green. Add in the greens as full leaves or chop them up into finer pieces to create a chopped salad.

Cheese:
Many of the salads call for a cheese that fits your diet preference. You'll be guided through a choice of dairy-free cheese, fat-free cheese, or vegan cheese and able to pick one that works for you. Feel free to mix it up, mix and match to create a salad that best fits your needs.

Grains:
I find that adding grains to my salads keeps me feeling full longer and not snacking in between meals. I like to add a grain such as rice, pasta, or potatoes to my salad bowls.

What type of rice can I use?
When a recipe calls for rice, choose from white rice, brown rice, or cauliflower rice. Feel free to use lentil rice or other riced vegetables. A combination of white or brown rice mixed with cauliflower rice will give you a low-carb salad option.

Want to save time?
To save time, use instant microwavable rice or frozen rice. You can also make your own the same day, or use any leftover rice you already have made in your fridge. The key to adding rice to these salads, though, is for you to have already prepared the rice before making this recipe to save time! If the rice has been refrigerated, warm for 30 to 60 seconds in the microwave or set out until the rice reaches room temperature.

Protein and Vegan Options:
Finally, choose to top off your salad with a lean protein such as grilled chicken or turkey, crispy protein such as chicken tenders, or completely skip the meat. Many salads give easy gluten-free and vegan meat substitutes such as vegan/gluten-free chick'n, crispy air-fried potatoes, vegetable tots, or ground up tater tots into a ground "meat"!

The Ultimate Buffalo Chicken Pasta Salad

Yield: 1 family-sized salad perfect for sharing

Gluten-free | Nut-free
Options: Dairy-free | Low-fat | Vegan

What you'll need:

1 box gluten-free pasta

3-4 tablespoon ranch

¼ cup quartered tomatoes

3 tablespoons feta

2 tablespoons diced fresh chives

2 cups gluten-free chicken tenders (page 126)

2 tablespoons Two-Ingredient Spicy Buffalo
Sauce (page 33)

Dairy-free option: Use vegan/dairy-free
feta and vegan/dairy-free ranch

Low-fat option: Use fat-free feta and fat-
free or low-fat ranch. Use grilled chicken
instead of crispy chicken tenders.

Vegan option: Use vegan/dairy-free feta
and vegan/dairy-free ranch. Use vegan/
gluten free chick'n fingers instead of
gluten-free chicken tenders.

Need a show-stopping side dish for your next BBQ or cookout? Look no further than this spicy pasta salad. This buffalo chicken pasta salad is always a hit when I bring it to a get-together. Everyone loves that the salad is only seven ingredients but packs a huge flavor. The crispy chicken gives the salad a variety of textures and helps soak up the spicy sauce!

What to do:

Bring a pot of water to a boil and cook pasta uncovered for approximately 7 to 10 minutes, or until pasta is fully cooked. Drain and let pasta chill for 30 minutes in the refrigerator.

Once cooled, mix pasta, vegan ranch dressing, tomatoes, feta, and chives together in a separate bowl.

Next, cut the gluten-free chicken tenders into 1-inch pieces. Mix chicken with buffalo sauce in a separate bowl. Then, add buffalo chicken to the top of the pasta salad.

Mix together carefully so as to not bread the cooked pasta. Chill for 30 more minutes and then serve!

Save Some Time

- The pasta can be made ahead of time and stored in the refrigerator for 2 to 3 days.
- Make the gluten-free chicken cutlets 2 to 3 days in advance.

Growing up, my family did not eat a lot of steak. My mom didn't eat red meat, so she just really didn't make it much. As an adult, though, I found that I actually do like a lean, thinly sliced steak, especially on a salad. This healthy but loaded steak salad is full of cheese and vegetables and topped with a homemade chimichurri vinaigrette. The vinaigrette is simple, easy to whip up, and the best part about this recipe is you likely have all these dried spices already in your kitchen!

Dairy-free option: Use vegan/dairy-free feta

Low-carb option: Use either brown rice or a combination of brown rice and cauliflower rice. Feel free to reduce the amount of rice from 1 cup to only a ½ cup for an ultra low-carb option.

Low-fat option: Use fat-free feta. Use a lean cut of steak.

Steak Salad
with Easy Chimichurri Vinaigrette

Yield: 1 salad

Gluten-free | Nut-free
Options: Dairy-free | Low-carb | Low-fat

For your base:

2 cups arugula, butter lettuce, romaine, green leaf lettuce, or any other leafy green

For your topping:

4 ounces London broil or sirloin tip steak or steak of your choice

2 tablespoons feta

¼ cup diced tomatoes

2 tablespoons diced red onion

1 bell pepper, any color

½ tablespoon olive oil

For your carb or grain:

1 cup fully cooked white rice OR

1 cup fully cooked brown rice OR

½ cup brown rice mixed with ½ cup cauliflower rice

For the dressing:

1 tablespoon red wine vinegar

1 tablespoon olive oil

1 tablespoon balsamic

½ teaspoon oregano

½ teaspoon salt

½ teaspoon pepper

½ teaspoon parsley

½ teaspoon garlic

½ teaspoon red pepper flakes

What to do
Cook the steak
Preheat your air fryer grill or outdoor grill. Grill your steak until it reaches 145°F or desired temperature. Let rest for at least 3 minutes before slicing. On a cutting board, cut the steak into thin slices. The thinner the better. Set aside.

Choose your leafy base
Add 2 cups of your chosen leafy green to your salad bowl.

Add toppings
Add steak slices to your salad bowl. Top with feta, diced tomatoes, spinach, arugula, and diced red onion. On a cutting board, cut pepper into 1-inch slices. Add the pepper slices to a frying pan with olive oil. Sauté on medium heat for 6 to 8 minutes until the peppers are soft and fully cooked. Thicker peppers will take a few minutes longer to cook. Add sautéed peppers to the salad bowl. Add rice.

Dress the salad
Add all the dressing ingredients to a small bowl and mix until fully combined. Mixture should be smooth like a salad dressing. Top salad with dressing, toss, and serve!

I love a good taco salad, but sometimes ground meat isn't my thing! If you're like me and want to skip the ground meat, one of my favorite substitutes is ground up tater tots sautéed in a pan with taco seasoning until they are browned and crispy. The texture mimics ground meat without having to use meat, and you can make it really crispy. It's a fantastic vegan option I use throughout the cookbook for anyone choosing to skip the meat or keep the recipe vegan.

Want more protein? In a frying pan, add ¼ pound of lean ground turkey or ground chicken, low-sodium taco seasoning, and ½ tablespoon oil of choice. Pan-fry on medium to medium-high heat until the ground meat is fully cooked and edges are crispy!

Taco Salad
with Avocado Crema

Yield: 1 salad

Gluten-free | Nut-free | Vegetarian
Options: Dairy-free | Lower-fat | Vegan

For your base:

2 cups arugula, butter lettuce, romaine, green leaf lettuce, or any other leafy green

For your toppings:

1 cup gluten-free tater tots

2 tablespoons low-sodium taco seasoning

½ tablespoon oil of choice

¼ cup corn

¼ cup black beans

¼ cup cherry tomatoes

2 tablespoons feta

For the dressings:

¼ cup salsa, salsa verde, or any other flavored salsa including mango salsa or chipotle salsa

¼ cup Vegan Avocado Crema (page 24)

Dairy-free option: Use vegan/dairy-free feta

Lower-fat option: Use fat-free feta

Vegan option: Use vegan/dairy-free feta

What to do:

Make the tater tot vegan "meat"

If tater tots are frozen, place in a microwave-safe bowl and warm in increments of 30 seconds until tots are room temperature. Next, crush tater tots with a fork until they are fully ground. The tater tots should be crushed into tiny pieces and should resemble the look of ground meat. In a frying pan, add the crushed tater tots, low-sodium taco seasoning, and ½ tablespoon oil of choice. Pan-fry on medium to medium-high heat until the tater tot pieces are of desired crispiness, approximately 7 to 11 minutes.

Choose your leafy base

Add 2 cups of your chosen leafy green to your salad bowl.

Add toppings

Add the corn and black beans to the salad bowl. On a cutting board, quarter the cherry tomatoes. Add to the salad bowl, along with the feta.

Dress the salad

Dress salad with desired salsa and ¼ cup Vegan Avocado Crema. Toss and serve!

Greek Salad
with a Quick + Healthy Tzatziki

Yield: 1 salad

Gluten-free | Nut-free
Options: Dairy-free | Low-carb | Low-fat | Vegan | Vegetarian

For your base:

2 cups arugula, butter lettuce, romaine, green leaf lettuce, or any other leafy green

For your carb or grain:

1 cup fully cooked white rice OR

1 cup fully cooked brown rice OR

½ cup brown rice mixed with ½ cup cauliflower rice

For your toppings:

½ cup cucumbers, diced

2 tablespoons olives

2 tablespoons sun-dried tomatoes

⅓ cup roasted red peppers, diced (jarred or sautéed at home)

2 tablespoons feta

salt and pepper, to taste

Dairy-free option: Use vegan/dairy-free feta

Low-carb option: Use either brown rice or a combination of brown rice and cauliflower rice. Feel free to reduce the amount of rice from 1 cup to only a ½ cup for an ultra low-carb option.

Low-fat option: Sub grilled chicken for chicken fingers. Use fat-free feta.

Vegan option: Use vegan/dairy-free feta. Use vegan/gluten-free chick'n.

Vegetarian option: Use vegan chick'n or skip the meat altogether

For your protein:

2–4 gluten-free chicken fingers

For your dressing:

Homemade Tzatziki (page 27)

This quick and healthy Greek salad is a go-to weekday meal in my house! It's fresh and packed with vegetables. You can choose from any leafy green base, top it off with a grain, a protein, and some easy homemade tzatziki!

What to do:

Make the protein or vegan protein

Air-fry the chicken fingers or chick'n on 390°F until the edges are browned and crispy. Make sure they are fully cooked inside. Once they are fully cooked and crispy, remove from the air fryer, cut into 1-inch cubes, and set aside.

Choose your leafy base

Add 2 cups of your chosen green to your salad bowl.

Add toppings

Add the rice, cucumbers, olives, sun-dried tomatoes, roasted red peppers, and feta to the salad bowl. Add the crispy chicken fingers.

Dress the salad

Dress salad with ¼ cup Homemade Tzatziki (page 27). Drizzle more olive oil on top, if desired. Add salt and pepper, to taste. Toss and serve!

Crispy Buffalo Caesar Salad

Yield: 1 salad

Gluten-free | Nut-free
Options: Dairy-free | Lower-carb | Low-fat | Vegan

For your base:

2 cups arugula, butter lettuce, romaine, green leaf lettuce, or any other leafy green

For your carb or grain:

⅓ cup fully cooked white rice OR

⅓ cup fully cooked brown rice OR

⅓ cup brown rice mixed with cauliflower rice

For your toppings:

½ cup tomato, diced

½ cup cucumbers, diced

½ an avocado, sliced

2 tablespoons feta

For your dressing:

2–3 tablespoons Caesar salad dressing (creamy works better than a vinaigrette)

What you'll need for the buffalo potatoes:

1½ cups Yukon gold potatoes, cut into ½-inch cubes

3 tablespoons Two-Ingredient Spicy Buffalo Sauce (page 33)

Dairy-free option: Use vegan/dairy-free feta and vegan/dairy-free Caesar salad dressing

Lower-carb option: Use either brown rice or a combination of brown rice and cauliflower rice. Feel free to reduce the amount of rice from 1 cup to only a ½ cup for an ultra low-carb option.

Low-fat option: Use fat-free feta and sub Caesar salad vinaigrette or low-fat Caesar dressing

Vegan option: Use vegan/dairy-free feta and vegan/dairy-free Caesar salad dressing

This crispy buffalo Caesar salad is packed with greens, tomatoes, cucumbers, healthy fats from avocado, and crispy air-fried potatoes. The potatoes are made in the air fryer to ensure they aren't fried with oil or butter. The potatoes are also covered with buffalo sauce and then air-fried to give it a crispy texture and pop of spice instead of drenching the salad with something too spicy to handle. You get the perfect mix of that creamy Caesar salad taste with a hint of spicy buffalo. For a higher protein option, add one 6-ounce grilled chicken breast, sliced into ½-inch strips.

What to do:

Make the potatoes

First, add the potatoes to the air fryer and cook at 390°F degrees for 8 to 10 minutes. These potatoes

(Continued on next page)

will cook initially without any oil or seasoning. Remove potatoes, and in a separate bowl, toss with 3 tablespoons vegan buffalo sauce. Once fully coated, add potatoes back into the air fryer for another 5 to 7 minutes until the edges are golden brown and the potatoes are fully cooked. Once finished, set aside.

Choose your leafy base
Add 2 cups of your chosen leafy green to your salad bowl.

Add toppings
Add the warm, fully cooked rice, tomato, cucumbers, avocado slices, and feta to the salad bowl. Top with crispy potatoes.
   Add dressing. Toss and serve!

Save Some Time

- Prepare the potatoes ahead of time and store them in an airtight container in the refrigerator for up to 3 days. When ready to make the salad, heat the potatoes in the air fryer on 390°F for 5 to 7 minutes to give them back their crispness before adding them to the salad.
- Prepare the vegetables ahead of time by slicing the tomatoes, cucumbers, and greens. Store them in an airtight container in the refrigerator for up to 3 days. Add a paper towel into the container to help control the moisture until you are ready to eat.

Asian Chicken Salad
with Sesame Carrot Fries

Yield: 1 salad

Gluten-free | Dairy-free | Nut-free
Option: Vegan/vegetarian

For your salad:

2 cups arugula, butter lettuce, romaine, green leaf lettuce, or any other leafy green

1 large carrot

½ tablespoon sesame oil

½ teaspoon ground ginger

½ teaspoon garlic powder

¼ cup diced cucumbers

½ cup mandarin oranges, canned or jarred

½ cup white rice or brown rice (fully cooked)

For your potential protein:

1 cup gluten-free chicken tenders (page 126)

For your dressing:

Creamy Asian Dressing (page 32)

Vegan/vegetarian option: Sub vegan/gluten-free chick'n tenders

Who said you can't put french fries in a salad? This Asian chicken salad is packed with flavor, and the best part is that it's also packed with sesame carrot fries. The carrot fries are air-fried to crispy perfection, and you might even make more for an extra side of fries to snack on!

What to do:

Add 2 cups of your chosen leafy green to your salad bowl.

Peel the carrot. On a cutting board, slice the carrot in half horizontally. Then, slice vertically into 1-inch strips to get french fry–like pieces. Add to a medium-sized bowl with sesame oil, ginger, and garlic. Toss to cover carrot fries with seasoning. Add to the air fryer and cook on 390°F degrees for 10 to 12 minutes or until fries are browned along the edges.

Add carrot, diced cucumbers, mandarin oranges, and fully cooked rice to the salad bowl. Rice should be cooked beforehand and warm or room temperature. Slice up the chicken tenders into ½-inch pieces and add to salad.

Add dressing. Toss and serve!

Crispy Chicken Honey Mustard Salad

Yield: 1 salad

Gluten-free
Options: Dairy-free | Lower-fat | Vegan

For your gluten-free herb croutons:
2 slices gluten-free bread or bread of choice
1 tablespoon garlic and herb seasoning
light oil spray

For your base:
2 cups arugula, butter lettuce, romaine, green
  leaf lettuce, or any other leafy green

For your toppings:
¼ avocado, sliced
¼ cup cucumber, diced
½ cup tomatoes, diced
6 slices of turkey pepperoni
⅓ cup gluten-free herb croutons

For your potential protein:
1 cup gluten-free chicken tenders, cut into
  ½-inch pieces (page 126)

For your dressing:
Honey Mustard Vinaigrette (page 29)

What to do:
Make the croutons
Cut 2 slices of gluten-free bread into ½-inch cubes. Spray with light oil spray. Top with garlic and herb seasoning. Air-fry on 390°F until crispy.

Choose your leafy base
Add 2 cups of your chosen leafy green to your salad bowl.

Add toppings
Top the salad with the avocado slices, diced cucumbers, and diced tomatoes. Add the 6 slices of turkey pepperoni to the air fryer. Air-fry on 390°F for 3 to 6 minutes until turkey pepperoni is crispy and crunchy. Remove and let rest on a paper towel for 2 minutes to absorb any extra oil. Crumble and add to salad. Add the gluten-free chicken tender and the croutons.

Add Honey Mustard Vinaigrette dressing. Toss and serve!

Dairy-free option: Make sure your bread for the croutons is dairy-free
Lower-fat option: Instead of chicken tenders, use one 6-ounce grilled chicken breast or feel free to skip the avocado (note: avocados do have a ton of good fat!)
Vegan option: Skip the pepperoni. Skip the chicken tenders and use vegan/gluten-free chick'n tenders instead. Make sure your bread for the croutons is vegan.

Save Some Time

Skip making the gluten-free chicken tenders and buy premade chicken tenders! They come in frozen as well as refrigerated options. You can also buy ones breaded in cauliflower instead of breadcrumbs. Heat them up in the air fryer on 390°F until the edges are golden brown. Once cooked, continue to cut into ½-inch pieces and add to salad.

Chopped Italian Goddess Salad

Yield: 1 salad

Gluten-free | Nut-free
Options: Dairy-free | Lower-fat

For your salad:

6 slices chicken or turkey cold cuts

15 slices mini turkey pepperoni

2 cups butter lettuce or romaine lettuce

¼ cup banana peppers

¼ cup roasted red peppers

2 tablespoons olives

¼ cup cucumbers

2 tablespoons red onion

2 slices provolone

For your dressing:

1 tablespoon red wine vinegar

1 tablespoon balsamic vinaigrette

2 teaspoons mayo

½ teaspoon oregano

½ teaspoon salt

½ teaspoon pepper

½ teaspoon garlic

Dairy-free option: Use dairy-free or vegan provolone for dairy-free recipe

Lower-fat option: Use fat-free or low-fat mayo. Use low-fat cheese.

Who doesn't love an Italian hero!? I always crave the flavor profiles of that sandwich; packed with pepperoni, turkey, banana peppers, and mayo but without any of the bread. But if you're like me and looking to taste the same flavors in a healthy lunch situation, this one's for you!

What to do:

For the salad

Chop all ingredients as small as you can! The smaller the better to create the perfect chopped salad. The best part about this is getting the perfect mixture of every ingredient in every bite. Add all chopped ingredients to a bowl.

For the dressing

Add all ingredients to a bowl and mix until fully combined. Mixture should be smooth like a salad dressing. Top with salad dressing and toss.

Chill for 2 hours before serving.

Typical comfort food consists of creamy dishes, warm meals, and recipes that stick to your bones . . . but one meal that doesn't fit this description is a Caesar salad. Hands down, Caesar salad fits into the comfort-food category. Whether it's the middle of the summer or deep in the winter, if I'm craving a Caesar salad, then I'm having a Caesar salad. It's as simple as that. For this ultimate Caesar salad, you start off with leafy greens, top them with homemade crunchy croutons, and seal the deal with a light Caesar vinaigrette dressing. You can choose to elevate this recipe by adding a little extra protein!

The Ultimate Caesar Salad
with Herbed Croutons

Yield: 1 salad

Gluten-free | Low-fat
Options: Dairy-free | Low-carb | Vegan | Potential protein

What you'll need:

2 slices gluten-free bread or bread of choice

light oil spray

2 cups romaine lettuce

1 tablespoon grated parmesan

2 tablespoons light Caesar vinaigrette dressing

1 tablespoon garlic and herb seasoning

Dairy-free option: Use dairy free/vegan Caesar dressing and dairy-free/vegan parmesan cheese

Low-carb option: Skip the croutons

Vegan option: Use dairy-free/vegan Caesar dressing and dairy-free/vegan parmesan cheese. Make sure to use vegan bread.

Potential protein: For a little extra protein, add grilled chicken, salmon, or chicken sausage. You can even choose to add vegan/gluten-free chick'n!

What to do:

Make the croutons

Cut 2 slices of gluten free bread into ½-inch cubes. Spray with light oil spray. Top with garlic and herb seasoning. Air-fry on 390°F until crispy. Set aside.

Prepare your leafy base

Add 2 cups of romaine lettuce to the salad bowl.

Add toppings

Top the salad with croutons, parmesan cheese, and grilled chicken.

Add Caesar dressing. Toss and serve!

Three combinations to elevate this salad:

Healthy protein twist

Add one 6-ounce chicken breast, grilled with salt, pepper, garlic, and onion powder. Make your own grilled chicken by grilling until the internal temperature of the chicken reaches 165°F. To save time, buy premade grilled chicken from any grocery store deli counter, premade section, or salad bar.

Pizza crouton twist

You'll need 1 to 2 slices of gluten-free pizza. Cut pizza into ½-inch pieces. Top with garlic and herb seasoning. Air-fry or bake at 390°F until crispy. Let sit for 10 minutes before adding to the salad.

Pasta salad twist

Add ½ cup gluten-free pasta (cooked and cooled).

Tex-Mex Chicken Salad
with Spicy Ranch Dressing

Yield: 1 salad

Gluten-free | Nut-free
Options: Dairy-free | Lower-fat | Vegan

What you'll need:

2 corn tortillas

½ tablespoon low-sodium taco seasoning

½ tablespoon oil of choice

2 cups butter lettuce or romaine lettuce, chopped

For potential protein:

1 (6-ounce) chicken breast

1 tablespoon low-sodium taco seasoning

For the toppings:

⅓ cup diced red peppers

¼ cup corn

¼ cup black beans

1 tablespoon feta

For the dressing:

½ tablespoon low-sodium taco seasoning

2 tablespoons ranch

Dairy-free option: Use vegan/dairy-free feta and vegan/dairy-free ranch

Lower-fat option: Use fat-free feta

Vegan option: Skip the chicken or use vegan/gluten-free chick'n. Use vegan/dairy-free feta and vegan/dairy-free ranch.

This spicy Tex-Mex salad has the perfect simple southwestern ranch dressing. It's only 2 ingredients: ranch and taco seasoning! It's so easy to substitute a fat-free ranch or a vegan ranch and you'd never know the difference. I use this dressing on salads, to dip fresh vegetables in, and on top of sandwiches!

What to do:

Make the crispy tortillas strips

To make the crispy tortillas strips, slice 2 corn tortillas into ½-inch strips. Add to frying pan with ½ tablespoon low-sodium taco seasoning and ½ tablespoon oil. Pan-fry until tortilla strips are crispy. Set aside and let cool before adding to salad.

Prepare your leafy base

Add 2 cups of butter or romaine lettuce to the salad bowl.

Make the chicken

Cover 1 chicken breast with 1 tablespoon of low-sodium taco seasoning. Make sure the seasoning is evenly distributed. Grill chicken for 8 to 10 minutes until the inside temperature reaches 165°F. Remove from the grill. Let sit for 4 to 5 minutes. Slice into 1-inch strips.

Add toppings

Top with peppers, corn, black beans, feta, and sliced grilled chicken. Add crispy tortilla strips.

For the dressing

Mix together ranch and ½ tablespoon low-sodium taco seasoning. Add dressing to salad. Toss and serve!

Everyday Black Bean Salad
with Lemon Caesar Vinaigrette

Yield: 1 salad

Gluten-free | Nut-free
Options: Dairy-free | Low-carb | Low-fat | Vegan

For your crispy taco potatoes:

1½ cups cubed (½-inch) Yukon gold potatoes

½ tablespoon low-sodium taco seasoning

Light cooking spray

For your salad:

2 cups butter lettuce or romaine lettuce, chopped

For your potential protein:

1 (6-ounce) grilled chicken breast

1 tablespoon low-sodium taco seasoning

For your toppings:

⅓ cup diced red peppers

¼ cup corn

¼ cup black beans

1 tablespoon feta

For your dressing:

2 tablespoons light Caesar vinaigrette salad dressing

½ tablespoon low-sodium taco seasoning

1 tablespoon fresh lemon juice

Dairy-free option: Use vegan/dairy-free feta and vegan/dairy-free Caesar vinaigrette

Low-carb option: Skip the potatoes!

Low-fat option: Use fat-free feta

Vegan option: Skip the chicken or use vegan/gluten-free chick'n. Use vegan/dairy-free feta and vegan/dairy-free Caesar vinaigrette.

I'm a sucker for a Caesar salad, especially this one with its taco flair and crispy potatoes! This salad is a combination of a taco salad and a Caesar salad while still being healthy and dietary friendly! It's super easy to make dairy free, vegan, low carb, and/or low fat! The crispy potatoes are the perfect taco crunch for a fresh and healthy lunch.

What to do:

Make the potatoes

Add potatoes to a medium-sized bowl. Spray with cooking spray. Add taco seasoning and toss. Once fully coated, add potatoes into the air fryer and cook on 390°F for 9 to 11 minutes until the edges are golden brown and the potatoes are fully cooked. Once finished, set aside.

Prepare your leafy base

Add 2 cups of chopped butter or romaine lettuce to the salad bowl.

Make the chicken

Cover 1 chicken breast with 1 tablespoon of low-sodium taco seasoning. Make sure the seasoning is evenly distributed. Grill chicken for 8 to 10 minutes until the inside temperature reaches 165°F. Remove from the grill. Let sit for 4 to 5 minutes. Slice into 1-inch strips.

Add toppings

Top with peppers, corn, black beans, feta, and sliced grilled chicken. Add the crispy potatoes.

For the dressing

Mix together Caesar dressing, lemon juice, and ½ tablespoon low-sodium taco seasoning. Add dressing to salad. Toss and serve!

10 Easy Arugula Salads
with a Clean Olive Oil Dressing

Yield: 1 salad or 2 side salads

Gluten-free | Nut-free
Options: Dairy-free | Vegan

For your salad base:

2 cups arugula or fresh spinach

1 tablespoon shaved parmesan cheese

For your simple dressing:

2 tablespoons oil of choice (I recommend olive oil here!)

salt and pepper, to taste

1 squeeze of lemon juice, optional

Dairy-free option: Use dairy-free/vegan cheese

Vegan option: Use any plant-based chick'n, plant-based chick'n tenders, or plant-based sausage, or nix the meat altogether. Use dairy-free/vegan cheese.

This super simple salad is perfect for on the go. It's easy to prepare ahead of time to bring to work or just to make your life easier. It's the perfect side salad option for a pasta dinner. This salad includes only oil, salt, and pepper for dressing, which makes this one of my absolute favorite clean-eating recipes! Feel free to top with a quick fresh squeeze of lemon juice! Plus, the best part: you can choose from any of the topping combinations below to create a new salad every time.

What to do:

Load up a bowl with the arugula or spinach base. Top the arugula with parmesan cheese. Top with oil of choice, salt, and pepper. Toss all ingredients together and select from any of the combinations on the next page to make this your own!

10 Combinations to Make the Arugula Salad Your Own

Grilled Chicken and Tomato
Add one 6-ounce grilled chicken breast sliced into 1-inch strips + ¼ cup sun-dried tomatoes, jarred in oil. (Make your own grilled chicken by grilling until the internal temperature of the chicken reaches 165°F degrees. To save time, buy premade grilled chicken from any grocery store deli counter, prepared section, or salad bar.)

Herbed Crouton and Prosciutto
Add ¼ cup gluten-free herbed croutons (page 97) + 1 tablespoon diced red onion + 3–4 slices of prosciutto!

Caprese
Add ½ cup fresh tomato slices + ¼ cup gluten-free herbed croutons (page 97) + ½ cup fresh mozzarella pearls (sub vegan/dairy-free mozzarella if needed)

Pear and Prosciutto
Slice 1 pear into ¼-inch thick slices and sauté with light cooking spray on medium heat until browned. Add sautéed pear slices to salad + 1 tablespoon diced red onion + 3–4 slices of prosciutto!

Avocado and Crispy Chickpea
Add ½ avocado into thin slices + toss chickpeas with oil, salt, pepper, and garlic and air-fry on 390°F until desired crispiness (I like them fully browned and extra crispy!).

Warm Pasta and Sausage
Add ¼ cup sun-dried tomatoes (jarred in oil) + ½ cup gluten-free pasta (cooked and cooled) + ¼ cup roasted chicken sausage

Avocado and Mozzarella
Cut ½ avocado into thin slices + ¼ cup sun-dried tomatoes + ½ cup fresh mozzarella pearls (sub vegan/dairy-free mozzarella if needed) + 1 tablespoon diced red onion

Butternut Squash and Feta
Add 2 tablespoons pumpkin seeds + 1 tablespoon diced red onion + 2 tablespoons fat free or vegan feta + ½ cup roasted butternut squash

Corn and Feta
Add 2 tablespoons corn + 1 tablespoon diced red onion + 2 tablespoons fat-free or vegan feta

Avocado and Grapefruit
Cut ½ avocado into thin slices + ½ grapefruit, sliced + 1 tablespoon diced red onion + 2 tablespoons fat-free or vegan feta

Light and Fresh Summer Salad
with Feta and Meatballs

Yield: 1 salad

Gluten-free | Nut-free
Options: Dairy-free | Low-carb | Low-fat

For your meatballs:

½ pound ground chicken or ground turkey

¼ cup gluten-free breadcrumbs

2 tablespoons egg whites

½ teaspoon salt

½ teaspoon pepper

½ teaspoon garlic powder

1 tablespoon plant-based milk

For your salad:

½ avocado

2 cups chopped broccoli slaw

¼ cup diced cucumbers

2 tablespoons diced red onion

2 tablespoons feta

2 tablespoons dried cherries

For your dressing:

Honey Mustard Vinaigrette (page 29) or
    Grapefruit Mustard Vinaigrette (page 28)

Dairy-free option: Use vegan/dairy-free
    feta

Low-carb option: Use pork rind
    breadcrumbs (naturally gluten-free)
    instead of gluten-free bread-based
    breadcrumbs

Low-fat option: Use fat-free feta. Omit the
    avocado (although avocados are packed
    with healthy fat!).

This salad is perfect for warm, summer dinners outside . . . but I also make this salad for lunch in the dead of winter when I'm desperately missing the summer weather. This salad is packed with fresh vegetables and topped with healthy meatballs that are air-fried instead of pan-fried with oil. The salad is topped with either a tangy grapefruit vinaigrette or a smooth honey mustard vinaigrette.

What to do:

Make the meatballs

In a bowl, combine the ground meat, breadcrumbs, egg whites, salt, pepper, garlic, and plant-based milk. After all the ingredients are fully combined, use an ice cream scoop or ¼ cup measuring cup to portion the meatballs. Roll meatballs in a circular motion in your hand until they form a smooth, round shape. Meatballs will be soft and wet but should still stick together.

Preheat the air fryer to 390°F. Add meatballs to the air fryer basket. Cook for 10 to 12 minutes until the meat is fully cooked, crispy, and browned on the outside and no longer pink in the center. Use a meat thermometer to check the interior temperature; look for 160°–165°F. Once they are fully cooked, set aside and prepare salad.

Prepare your salad base

Add 2 cups of broccoli slaw to the salad bowl.

Add toppings

On a cutting board, slice the avocado in half, remove the skin and pit, and cut into 1-inch cubes. Add the avocado, diced cucumbers, red onion, feta, and dried cherries. Toss and top with meatballs.

Add Honey Mustard Vinaigrette or Grapefruit Mustard Vinaigrette and serve!

Avocado Chicken Salad

Yield: 3 cups

Gluten-free | Nut-free
Options: Dairy-free | Low-fat

What you'll need:

1 large ripe avocado

¼ cup Greek yogurt

2 tablespoons grated parmesan cheese

1 teaspoon salt

1 teaspoon pepper

1 teaspoon garlic

2 cups shredded chicken

Dairy-free option: Use vegan/dairy-free yogurt and vegan/dairy-free parmesan cheese

Low-fat option: Use fat-free plain Greek yogurt

Save Some Time

To save time, instead of making chicken at home and shredding it, buy a rotisserie chicken from the grocery store and easily shred the chicken yourself. Note that a warm rotisserie chicken is easier to shred than a refrigerated one, so I prefer to shred the rotisserie chicken as soon as I get home. Store the shredded chicken in an airtight container for 1 to 3 days in the refrigerator until you are ready to use it.

I first had an avocado chicken salad at a food festival in New York City. It was served stuffed inside a warm corn arepa. Literally at first bite I was hooked. I made a few trial-and-error batches and taste-tested them until I came up with the recipe that was closest to what I had tasted at the food festival—but still healthy and guilt free!

What to do:

Cut the avocado in half, remove the skin and pit. Add to a large bowl. With a fork, mash the avocado. There should be no lumps or large pieces of avocado. This should look smooth, like guacamole. Add the yogurt, parmesan cheese, salt, pepper, and garlic. Mix together until fully combined. Next, fold in the shredded chicken. Refrigerate for 1 hour before serving.

This avocado chicken salad can be served in a bowl with crackers or pretzels on the side for scooping. You can serve the salad with corn chips, as well. Feel free to add on top of a bed of greens, or on top of gluten-free toast, gluten-free bagel, gluten-free English muffin, or any other gluten-free carb you enjoy. You can also slice up a polenta log and air-fry the slices until they're crispy and the edges are brown. Then add 2 tablespoons of avocado salad on top of each round for a bite-sized snack!

Crispy Chicken, Goat Cheese, and Arugula Salad

Yield: 1 salad

Gluten-free | Nut-free
Options: Dairy-free | Vegan

For your salad:

2 cups arugula or baby arugula

3 tablespoons goat cheese

¼ cup diced tomatoes

¼ cup diced cucumbers

1 cup gluten-free chicken tenders (page 126)

For your dressing:

1½ tablespoons balsamic glaze or balsamic
   vinaigrette

1 tablespoon olive oil

½ teaspoon salt

½ teaspoon pepper

Dairy-free option: Use vegan/dairy-free
   goat cheese or any other soft vegan
   dairy-free cheese

Vegan option: Use vegan/dairy-free goat
   cheese and sub vegan chick'n tenders
   instead of gluten-free chicken tenders

Balsamic glaze and olive oil over arugula is one of the most refreshing salad combinations out there. It's perfect for a clean and healthy meal. This salad is easy to make, topped with only three easy ingredients, and with the gluten-free crispy chicken in it, you can bet you'll be making this again and again.

What to do:

Add 2 cups of arugula or baby arugula to your salad bowl. Add goat cheese, tomatoes, and cucumbers. Slice up the chicken tender into ½-inch pieces and add to salad.

Mix together the balsamic glaze, olive oil, salt, and pepper. Dress the salad. Toss and serve!

Sweet Potato and Ground Turkey Tacos (vegan option), page 110

Quick Meals for Lazy Weeknights

Weeknights are the hardest days to find time to cook a healthy meal. You're hungry and you're craving something really tasty after a full day of work, but you don't have two hours to prepare a dish. That's where this chapter comes in. All the recipes in this chapter are, of course, gluten-free, but they're healthy and packed with fresh vegetables and clean ingredients. Plus, each of these meals can be made in 30 minutes or fewer to free up the rest of your weeknight for much deserved relaxation time.

Sweet Potato and Ground Turkey Tacos

Yield: 2 servings (6 tacos)

Gluten-free | Dairy-free | Nut-free
Options: Lower-carb | Vegan

What you'll need:

1 pound ground turkey

1 tablespoon olive oil or oil of choice, divided

2 tablespoons garlic powder, divided

2 teaspoons cumin, divided

1 sweet potato

1½ tablespoons sugar-free maple syrup, honey, or agave

2 cups fresh spinach

¼ cup diced red onion

salt and pepper, to taste

6 corn tortillas

For your topping:

½ cup arugula

Vegan Avocado Crema (page 24)

Lower-carb option: Use cauliflower tortillas instead of corn tortillas! This won't be low-carb but will reduce the amount of carbs.

Vegan option: Use vegan/dairy-free feta. Omit ground turkey and add a second sweet potato.

What to do:

Make the ground turkey

In a frying pan, add the ground turkey, ½ tablespoon of olive oil, 1 tablespoon garlic powder, and 1 teaspoon cumin. Sauté on medium heat until turkey is browned and fully cooked.

Make the sweet potatoes

Slice the sweet potato into ½-inch cubes. In a separate frying pan, add the sweet potato cubes, honey, ½ tablespoon of olive oil, 1 tablespoon garlic powder, and 1 teaspoon cumin, spinach, and onions. Sauté on medium until sweet potatoes are fully cooked and vegetables are cooked down.

Prepare the tacos

Preheat oven to 350°F. Once preheated, add corn tortillas to a pan or straight on the rack and warm tortillas for 3 to 5 minutes. Tortillas should be warm but still soft so the tortillas are easier to work with. They should not be crispy. Remove corn tortillas from the oven and place onto a serving plate. Next, top each corn tortilla with ground turkey, spinach, onions, and sweet potatoes. Salt and pepper to taste. Top tacos with arugula and Vegan Avocado Crema.

Creamy Avocado Pasta

Yield: 2–3 meals

Gluten-free | Dairy-free | Nut-free | Vegan | Vegetarian
Options: Low-carb

For your sauce:

2 tablespoons minced garlic

¼ cup diced red onion

1 tablespoon olive oil or oil of choice

1 large ripe avocado or 2 ripe mini avocados,
    peeled and pit removed

½ teaspoon salt

½ teaspoon pepper

2 tablespoons lemon juice

3 tablespoons vegan parmesan cheese or
    nutritional yeast

¼ cup plant-based milk

You'll also need:

1 box gluten-free pasta

2 cups fresh spinach

1 cup arugula

¼ cup shaved parmesan

Low-carb option: Use zucchini noodles!

There's nothing like a healthy, guilt-free creamy pasta sauce! And I know what you're thinking: will this warm avocado cream sauce taste like warm guacamole? I promise you it does not! This sauce is creamy and garlicky with a hint of lemon juice! The avocado is a neutral taste that gives the sauce a creamy consistency without an overwhelming avocado flavor! If you want to add protein (thus, no longer a vegan/vegetarian option), add one 6-ounce grilled chicken breast sliced into ½-inch strips.

What to do:

Make the sauce

In a frying pan, sauté minced garlic, red onion, and ½ tablespoon olive oil on medium heat until onion is soft and translucent. Add to the blender. Add avocado, salt, pepper, lemon juice, parmesan cheese, and milk to the blender. Blend together all sauce ingredients until the sauce is smooth.

Make the pasta

Boil gluten-free pasta according to box directions. Drain pasta water from the pot but leave pasta.

Add sauce and spinach to the pasta pot. Warm on low heat for 2 to 4 minutes until sauce is warm and spinach is wilted. Remove from heat and plate.

Top with arugula and shaved parmesan and serve.

Clean-Out-Your-Fridge Turkey Soup

Yield: 8 servings

Gluten-free | Dairy-free | Low-fat | Nut-free

What you'll need:

1 large carrot, diced

2 cups fresh string beans, diced

1 small yellow or white onion, diced

2 tablespoons olive oil or oil of choice

1–2 tablespoons minced garlic

8 cups any kind of broth or stock (see below for options)

2 cups fresh shredded turkey or chicken

3 cups fresh spinach

1 cup grains (see below for options)

2 bay leaves

1 teaspoon dried parsley

salt and pepper, to taste

What grains can I use?

Use any type of gluten-free pasta, vegetable-based pasta, lentil pasta, brown rice, white rice, vegetable rice, etc.

What broth can I use?

Make this recipe your own and use any broth you'd like. Use chicken stock, turkey stock, bone broth, beef broth, vegetable stock, or mushroom broth.

I'm a huge fan of not letting any food go to waste! This soup is perfect for a clean-out-your-fridge day! You can use any vegetable, protein, or starch you have. It's cozy, warm, and a perfect healthy meal for days you're feeling lazy! This recipe can be prepared ahead of time to take to work or store the soup in the fridge for a rainy day. You can always add extra veggies you have, like peppers, or beans, chickpeas, etc.

What to do:

Add carrots, string beans, and onions to a soup pot with 2 tablespoons olive oil or oil of choice and minced garlic. Sauté until onions are clear, approximately 5 to 7 minutes. Add broth or stock. Bring to boil then turn down to simmer for 20 minutes with the lid on.

Next, add shredded turkey or chicken, spinach, grains, whole bay leaves, parsley, salt and pepper. Simmer until the grains are fully cooked. Pasta or veggie rice will be fully cooked by the end of the 10 to 12 minutes but brown/white rice will need to simmer for approximately 20 minutes total. Check the grains before removing from heat to make sure they are soft and cooked. Remove bay leaves before serving. Ladle the soup into individual bowls. If desired, top with dairy-free parmesan cheese and red pepper flakes.

Store in an airtight container in the refrigerator for 2 to 3 days or the freezer for up to 3 months. To reheat, add to pot on low to medium low heat and cook until warm.

Save Some Time

To save time, use leftover shredded turkey or chicken that you already have made. If you do not have any shredded protein, sub shredded chicken from a storebought rotisserie chicken.

Garlic and Herb Potato Tacos

Yield: 1 serving (3 tacos)

Gluten-free | Dairy-free | Vegetarian
Options: Lower-carb | Low-fat | Vegan

For your garlic herb potatoes:

1½ cups of Yukon gold potatoes

½ teaspoon garlic salt

½ teaspoon dried parsley

½ teaspoon onion powder

½ teaspoon dried oregano

½ teaspoon dried basil

½ teaspoon pepper

Light cooking spray

For your tacos:

3 corn tortillas

2 tablespoons roasted red peppers, diced
    (jarred or sautéed at home)

2 tablespoons feta

½ avocado, sliced

¼ cup arugula

2 tablespoons Red Pepper Aioli (page 30)

Lower-carb option: Use cauliflower tortillas instead of corn tortillas! The recipe won't be low-carb, but this will reduce the amount of carbs.

Low-fat option: Use fat-free feta

Vegan option: Use vegan/dairy-free feta

What to do:

Make the garlic herb potatoes

First, cut Yukon gold potatoes into ½-inch cubes. Add the cubes to a medium-sized bowl. Spray with light oil spray if needed for the seasoning to stick. Mix together until all cubes are evenly coated with seasoning. Add the seasoned potato cubes to the air fryer and cook at 390°F for 8 to 10 minutes. Add an extra 2 to 3 minutes for larger cubes.

Prepare the tacos

Preheat the oven to 350°F. Once preheated, add corn tortillas to a pan or straight on the rack and warm tortillas for 3 to 5 minutes. Tortillas should be warm but still soft so the tortillas are easier to work with. They should not be crispy. Remove corn tortillas from the oven and place onto a serving plate. Top each taco with roasted red pepper aioli, then add roasted garlic and herb potatoes. Top each taco with red peppers, feta, avocado slices, and arugula.

Buffalo Chicken Tacos
with Avocado Crema

Yield: 1 serving (3 tacos)

Gluten-free | Dairy-free | Low-fat
Options: Lower-carb | Vegan

What you'll need:

2–3 gluten-free chicken tenders (page 126)

2 tablespoons Two-Ingredient Spicy Buffalo
Sauce (page 33)

3 corn tortillas

For your topping:

½ cup tomatoes, diced

¼ cup red onion, diced

1 cup arugula

¼ cup Vegan Avocado Crema (page 24)

Lower-carb option: Use cauliflower tortillas
instead of corn tortillas! This recipe won't
be low carb, but this will reduce the
amount of carbs.

Vegan option: Instead of using chicken,
substitute air-fried buffalo sweet
potatoes (see below)

What to do:

Prepare the buffalo chicken

Cut gluten-free chicken tenders into 1-inch cubes.
Toss with buffalo sauce and add to the frying pan
or air fryer for 3 to 5 minutes to heat up. The
chicken should be fully cooked before this, so the
3 to 5 minutes are only to heat up the chicken with
the buffalo sauce.

Prepare the tacos

Preheat oven to 350°F. Once preheated, add corn
tortillas to a pan or straight on the rack and warm
tortillas for 3 to 5 minutes. Tortillas should be
warm but still soft so the tortillas are easier to work
with. They should not be crispy. Remove corn tortillas from the oven and place onto a serving plate.
Top each taco with buffalo chicken, red onion,
tomatoes, and arugula. Add a dollop of Vegan
Avocado Crema to each taco. Enjoy!

Sweet Potato Swap!

Slice a sweet potato into ½-inch cubes. Add the sweet potato cubes and buffalo sauce to a
medium bowl. Toss together until sweet potatoes are coated evenly. Add to the air fryer and
cook on 390°F for 8 to 10 minutes. Sweet potato cubes should be browned and crispy along the
edges but still soft in the center.

Butternut Squash Tacos
with Cranberry Aioli

Yield: 1 servings (3 tacos)

Gluten-free | Dairy-free | Nut-free | Vegetarian
Options: Lower-carb | Low-fat | Vegan

For your tacos:

½ cup butternut squash, cut into
　½-inch cubes

¼ cup cauliflower rice

2 tablespoons diced red onion

½ tablespoon olive oil or oil of choice

½ teaspoon cinnamon

½ teaspoon cumin

½ teaspoon cayenne pepper

¼ cup fresh spinach

3 corn tortillas

For your cranberry aioli:

1 tablespoon mayonnaise

1 tablespoon cranberry sauce

½ tablespoon olive oil

1 teaspoon maple syrup or honey

salt and pepper, to taste

> **Lower-carb option:** Use cauliflower tortillas instead of corn tortillas! The recipe won't be low-carb, but this will reduce the amount of carbs.
>
> **Low-fat option:** Use fat-free or low-fat mayo
>
> **Vegan option:** Use sugar-free maple syrup or agave and vegan mayo for the cranberry aioli

There is something about butternut squash and cranberry sauce that screams Thanksgiving! I developed this recipe after Thanksgiving when I was determined to find a recipe to use my leftover cranberry sauce. These tacos are heavy on the fall flavors but still light and healthy. These tacos will leave you wishing Thanksgiving came around once a month.

What to do:

Make the butternut squash and cauliflower hash

In a frying pan, add the butternut squash, cauliflower rice, red onion, olive oil, cinnamon, cumin, and cayenne pepper. Cook on medium heat for 3 to 5 minutes, then add spinach and continue to cook for another 7 to 10 minutes on medium heat until all veggies are fully cooked. The butternut squash will take the longest to cook, so once removed from the heat, make sure you are able to easily pierce the butternut squash cubes with a fork.

Prepare the cranberry aioli

While the squash and vegetables are cooking, add the mayo, cranberry sauce, olive oil, honey, salt, and pepper to a small bowl. Mix together until fully mixed and smooth. It's okay to use a food processor, if needed. Texture should look like a smooth cranberry-colored mayo.

Prepare the tacos

Preheat oven to 350°F. Once preheated, add corn tortillas to a pan or straight on the rack and warm tortillas for 3 to 5 minutes. Tortillas should be warm but still soft so the tortillas are easier to work with. They should not be crispy. Remove corn tortillas from the oven and place onto a serving plate. Add the squash and other vegetables and top each corn tortilla with the cranberry aioli.

Arugula Pesto Tacos

Yield: 1 serving (3 tacos)

Gluten-free | Nut-free
Options: Dairy-free | Lower-carb | Low-fat | Vegan

What you'll need:

3 corn tortillas

1 cup tater tot "meat" (page 16)

½ cup diced red onion

½ cup diced peppers

½ cup corn

3 tablespoons feta

¼ cup arugula

For your topping:

3 tablespoons Arugula Pesto Aioli (page 25)

Dairy-free option: Use vegan/dairy-free feta

Lower-carb option: Use cauliflower tortillas instead of corn tortillas! The recipe won't be low-carb, but this will the amount of carbs.

Low-fat option: Use fat-free feta

Vegan option: Use vegan/dairy-free feta

These tacos are an easy vegan meal packed with extra crunch and topped off with a quick pesto aioli. They definitely are a spin on traditional tacos since they are stuffed with potatoes, arugula, and pesto, but they still are topped with corn, peppers, and onions. They're gluten-free, nut-free, can be vegan, and you make them without any butter or oil so they are a healthy, low-fat meal option.

What to do:

Prepare the tacos

Preheat oven to 350°F. Once preheated, add corn tortillas to a pan or straight on the rack and warm tortillas for 3 to 5 minutes. Tortillas should be warm but still soft so the tortillas are easier to work with. They should not be crispy. Remove corn tortillas from the oven and place onto serving plate. Add 1 tablespoon Arugula Pesto Aioli to each taco. Top each taco with tater tot "meat," red onion, peppers, corn, feta, and arugula. Enjoy!

Roasted Vegetable Tacos
with Lemon Garlic Aioli

Yield: 1 serving (3 tacos)

Gluten-free | Nut-free | Vegetarian
Options: Dairy-free | Low-fat | Lower-carb | Vegan

What you'll need:

½ cup corn

½ cup diced red peppers

¼ cup diced white onion

½ teaspoon salt

½ teaspoon pepper

½ tablespoon olive oil or oil of choice or cooking spray

½ cup black beans

3 corn tortillas

For your topping:

3 tablespoons Lemon Garlic Aioli (page 26)

½ cup chopped fresh spinach

¼ cup diced cherry tomatoes

½ avocado, sliced

2 tablespoons feta

Dairy-free option: Use vegan/dairy-free feta

Low-fat option: Use fat-free feta

Lower-carb option: Use cauliflower tortillas instead of corn tortillas! The recipe won't be low-carb, but this will reduce the amount of carbs.

Vegan option: Use vegan/dairy-free feta

What to do:

In a frying pan, add corn, peppers, onions, salt, pepper, and oil. Sauté on medium heat for approximately 7 to 10 minutes until vegetables are fully cooked and slightly charred on the edges. Add black beans and continue to cook mixture for 1 extra minute to warm the beans.

Prepare the tacos

Preheat oven to 350°F. Once preheated, add corn tortillas to a pan or straight on the rack and warm tortillas for 3 to 5 minutes. Tortillas should be warm but still soft so the tortillas are easier to work with. They should not be crispy. Remove corn tortillas from the oven and place onto serving plate. Top each taco with 1 tablespoon of Lemon Garlic Aioli. Add cooked peppers, onions, corn, and black beans. Top with fresh chopped spinach, fresh diced tomatoes, avocado slices, and feta cheese! Enjoy!

Taco-Stuffed Sweet Potatoes

Yield: 1 serving (1 potato)

Dairy-free | Gluten-free | Nut-free | Vegan | Vegetarian

What you'll need:

½ cup corn

½ cup black beans

½ cup diced bell peppers

¼ cup diced white onions

1 tablespoon low-sodium taco seasoning

½ tablespoon olive oil, oil of choice, or cooking spray

1 large sweet potato

¼ cup diced tomatoes

For your topping:

2 tablespoons salsa

½ an avocado slices

3 tablespoons Vegan Avocado Crema (page 24)

What to do:

In a medium frying pan, add the corn, black beans, peppers, onions, taco seasoning, and oil. Cook vegetables on medium heat for 5 to 8 minutes or until vegetables are browned along the edges and the peppers and onions are soft. Turn down to lowest setting to keep warm until serving.

Prepare the sweet potato

Run the sweet potato under cold water so the outside doesn't get dried out when cooking. Then, using a fork, prick the sweet potato to create ventilation. In the microwave, cook the sweet potato until fully soft, approximately 5 to 6 minutes. If the sweet potato is not soft to the touch after 5 minutes, continue in 30-second increments until fully cooked.

Prepare the meal

Once the sweet potato is fully cooked, slice down the center and open. Don't hold your hand over the opening; pinch at the sides carefully and pull open so you don't burn yourself on the steam. Inside the opening, stuff with charred corn, beans, peppers, onions, and tomatoes. Top with salsa, avocado slices, and a heaping scoop of Avocado Crema! Enjoy!

Want to add some protein?

Add shredded chicken! To save time, instead of making chicken at home and shredding it, buy a rotisserie chicken from the grocery store and easily shred the chicken yourself. A warm rotisserie chicken is easier to shred than a refrigerated one, so I prefer to shred the rotisserie as soon as I get home and store the shredded chicken in an airtight container for 1 to 3 days in the refrigerator until you are ready to use it.

Easy Air-fried Chicken Fingers and French Fries

Yield: 3-4 chicken fingers & 15 fries (serves 2)

Gluten-free | Low-fat | Nut-free
Options: Dairy-free | Low-carb | Vegetarian

For your chicken fingers:

¾ cup egg whites

1 cup gluten-free breadcrumbs

1 cup pork rind crumbs or 1 cup rice flour or 1
   additional cup gluten-free breadcrumbs

1 cup grated parmesan cheese

½ teaspoon salt

½ teaspoon pepper

½ teaspoon garlic powder

½ teaspoon onion powder

½ teaspoon paprika

1 pound chicken breasts or chicken tenders

For your french fries:

2 large russet potatoes

½ teaspoon salt

½ teaspoon pepper

½ teaspoon garlic powder

½ teaspoon onion powder

½ teaspoon paprika

½ teaspoon parsley

½ tablespoon olive oil or oil of choice

For your topping:

Gold Rush Sauce (page 31) or Campfire Sauce
   (page 31)

Dairy-free option: Use vegan/dairy-free
   parmesan cheese

Low-carb option: Use pork rind
   breadcrumbs (naturally gluten-free)
   instead of gluten-free bread-based
   breadcrumbs

Vegetarian option: Breaded crispy zucchini
   fries: swap the chicken for 2 large
   zucchini!

When I was a kid, my go-to restaurant order was always chicken fingers. Even when I went to college, chicken fingers were still my favorite bar food to order. So, when I ended up going gluten-free, I was completely devastated. Of course, you can buy gluten-free chicken fingers at the grocery store, but do they ever really measure up to the restaurant version? No. So, I decided to make my own extra crispy, air-fried version. The chicken fingers aren't fried in oil and use egg whites instead of eggs, so they are a healthy version that gets extra crispy! They are perfect to eat by themselves or on top of any salad!

What to do:

For the chicken fingers

First, add egg whites to a bowl. Set aside. In a separate bowl, add gluten-free breadcrumbs, pork rinds, parmesan cheese, and spices. Mix together. Set bowls side by side. If you are using chicken breasts, you'll have to cut them into 2-inch strips. Preheat air fryer to 390°F.

Dip chicken tenders into the egg mixture first, then breadcrumbs mixture next. Make sure each tender is evenly coated with breadcrumbs, pressing the crumbs into the chicken to make sure they stick.

Once each chicken tender is prepared, add to air fryer basket. No tenders should be overlapping or touching. Space ½ inch apart so they don't stick. Next, spray the tenders lightly with cooking spray. Air-fry for 14 to 17 minutes until chicken is fully cooked. Check the interior temperature with a meat thermometer to make sure the chicken reaches 165°F. Chicken should not be pink inside. Outside coating should be evenly browned and crispy. Once fully cooked, remove from the air fryer, plate, and serve.

For the french fries
Preheat air fryer to 390°F. On a cutting board, cut potatoes in half horizontally.

Next, cut each piece vertically so the potato is cut into 1-inch strips resembling traditional french fry length and width. Add potatoes to a large bowl. Top fries with seasoning and olive oil or cooking spray. Toss so all fries are evenly covered with spices. Add french fries to the air fryer basket and cook for 5 minutes. Open the air fryer and toss the fries so they cook evenly. Continue cooking for another 5 to 8 minutes until desired crispiness is achieved. Remove, plate, and serve with sauce of choice!

Put your spin on things!
- To make sweet potato fries, swap the russet potatoes with 2 large sweet potatoes!
- To make polenta fries, swap the russet potatoes for a log of polenta!
- To make zucchini fries, swap the russet potatoes for 2 large zucchini!

Easy Taco Lasagna, page 140

Time-Saving Casseroles and Bakes

Sunday afternoons are meant for casseroles and meal prepping. I love a fall Sunday afternoon when football's on, a casserole is baking, and I'm planning my healthy meals for the week. If you're busy and on the go all week and just want a cozy meal to come home to, or you're working all week and want to prep a healthy bake for your lunch meal preps, this chapter has you covered with healthy but filling meals that will save you time during your busy week. These casseroles are filled with hearty rice or low-carb cauliflower rice options, shredded chicken for a lean protein, or jackfruit for a vegan option. Whatever your dietary need or preference is, these casseroles are about to make your week a heck of a lot easier!

Creamy Vegan Mac and "Cheese"

Plus 6 Easy Ways to Make It Your Own!

Yield: 4 servings

Gluten-free | Dairy-free | Nut-free | Vegan | Vegetarian

What you'll need:

1 (12-ounce) box gluten-free pasta

For your "cheese" sauce:

1 cup pumpkin puree, butternut squash puree, or sweet potato puree

1 cup plant-based milk

1 tablespoon coconut flour, gluten-free flour, or brown-rice flour

4 tablespoons vegan parmesan cheese or nutritional yeast

1 teaspoon Dijon mustard

1 teaspoon garlic

1 teaspoon onion powder

1 teaspoon paprika

1 teaspoon turmeric

½ teaspoon pepper

½ teaspoon salt

For your topping:

⅓ cup gluten-free breadcrumbs

1 teaspoon garlic powder

1 teaspoon onion powder

1 tablespoon olive oil or 1 tablespoon melted vegan butter

Andrew, my fiancé, and I both love this recipe, but we have very different opinions on the name! I love the creamy vegan sauce on this pasta! This recipe reminds me of mac and cheese based on the color and consistency of the sauce. Plus, any topping usually added to mac and cheese can be added here, as well! Andrew, on the other hand, still loves this recipe but thinks it should just be called exactly what it is: pasta with a creamy butternut squash sauce. I can't say he's wrong, but either way, it's a crowd pleaser in my household any day of the week, especially on a cold fall day when we just want to relax and eat all the comfort food we can.

What to do:

Preheat the oven to 350°F. Next, cook one box of gluten-free pasta.

While pasta is cooking, add vegetable puree, milk, flour, cheese/yeast, Dijon mustard, and spices to a separate bowl. Mix until fully combined. Sauce should be smooth and creamy and should resemble traditional mac and cheese sauce.

Add sauce to the bottom of a 9 × 9–inch dish. When pasta is done cooking, drain water and add to the dish with sauce. Carefully mix together until pasta is evenly covered with sauce.

In a separate bowl, mix together breadcrumbs and spices for topping. Sprinkle evenly over top. Add to a preheated oven and bake for approximately 30 to 40 minutes. Let sit for 3 to 5 minutes before serving! Enjoy!

(Continued on next page)

Save Some Time

Instead of topping with breadcrumbs, you can also top with mashed-up gluten-free cheese crackers or mashed-up gluten-free cheese crisps. Cheese crisps come in any cheese flavor such as parmesan, cheddar, etc. Any cheesy flavor will work!

6 Mix-In Combinations to Make This Mac and Cheese Your Own

Broccoli and Garlic
Add 2 cups diced broccoli and ½ tablespoon minced garlic into pasta mixture before baking.

Spicy Sausage
Add 2 cups diced spicy chicken sausage + ½ cup diced red bell peppers + ¼ cup diced red onion into the pasta mixture before baking. By adding sausage, this recipe is still delicious, but note this version is not vegan then.

Spinach and Onion
Add 2 cups fresh spinach + ¼ cup diced red onion + 2 extra tablespoons vegan parmesan cheese into pasta mixture before baking.

Buffalo Chicken
Add 2 cups gluten-free chicken tenders, cut into ½-inch pieces (page 126) + a drizzle of Two-Ingredient Spicy Buffalo Sauce (page 33) onto top of pasta mixture before baking. By adding buffalo chicken, this recipe is still delicious, but note this version of the recipe is not vegan then.

Loaded
Add vegan cheddar cheese shreds on top of pasta in a baking dish before baking. Top with 3 tablespoons bacon bits or vegan bacon bits + 3 tablespoons chives after baking. By adding bacon bites, this recipe is still delicious, but note this version of the recipe is not vegan then. Make sure to use vegan bacon bits if needed for a vegan recipe.

Spicy Taco
Add ¼ cup black beans + ¼ cup diced red onions + ¼ cup diced red bell peppers + 2 tablespoons taco seasoning into pasta mixture before baking. Add vegan cheddar cheese shreds on top of pasta before baking.

Healthier French Onion Soup

Yield: 5 cups

Gluten-free | Dairy-free | Low-fat | Nut-free
Options: Vegan/vegetarian

What you'll need:

2 white onions

½ teaspoon dried thyme

1 bay leaf

2 tablespoons vegan butter

½ cup white wine

4 cups chicken broth or mushroom broth

½ teaspoon salt

½ teaspoon pepper

Vegan/vegetarian option: Use the mushroom broth instead of the chicken broth

I used to judge every restaurant I went to by their French onion soup. Was the soup served in the little crocks? Was the cheese-to-broth ratio right? But those games ended when I went gluten-free because ordering soup out is risky business. You don't know if the chef used flour to thicken a soup. Also, I have yet to find a restaurant that gives you an option for gluten-free bread on top of your French onion soup. So, the right move was to make my own. It's healthier than what you'd normally get at a restaurant, plus it's gluten-free, dairy-free, and has an easy vegan substitution!

What to do:

On a cutting board, slice white onions into ½-inch strips. Add sliced onions, thyme, bay leaf, and butter to the bottom of a soup pot. Cook on medium-low heat until onions are fully caramelized, approximately 45 minutes.

Once onions are caramelized, add the wine. Continue cooking for 10 more minutes to cook out the alcohol. Add broth, salt, and pepper. Continue to cook on medium-low for approximately 30 to 45 more minutes.

Once soup is done, ladle 1 to 2 cups into personal-sized bowls.

Optional toppings

Add slices of gluten-free bread to a baking sheet. Top each slice with vegan mozzarella. Bake on 350°F until the bread is crispy and cheese is melted. I also like to use a crusty gluten-free baguette sliced into 1-inch thick slices. Add 1 slice to the top of each bowl of soup.

Healthier French Onion Soup and Easy French Onion Chicken Skillet, pages 133 and 135

Easy French Onion Chicken Skillet

Yield: 4 servings

Gluten-free | Nut-free
Option: Dairy-free | Low-fat

What you'll need:

3 cups Healthier French Onion Soup (page 133)

1 tablespoon olive oil

4 (4-ounce) grilled chicken breasts

1 teaspoon minced garlic

½ teaspoon salt

½ teaspoon pepper

1 cup vegan mozzarella or fat-free mozzarella

Dairy-free option: Use vegan mozzarella

Low-fat option: Use fat-free mozzarella

This French onion chicken skillet is perfect to make with leftover French onion soup! It's packed with French onion soup flavor, caramelized onions, and topped with warm cheese.

What to do:

Preheat the oven to 350°F.

Make gluten-free, dairy-free French onion soup (recipe 133).

Add 1 tablespoon olive oil to a cast-iron skillet. Place chicken into the cast-iron skillet. Brush minced garlic evenly on all the chicken pieces. Top with salt and pepper.

On the stovetop, brown chicken on both sides over medium-high heat, approximately 3 to 5 minutes on each side. Once chicken is browned, pour the French onion soup on top. Next, add dairy-free cheese on top of each chicken breast. Bake for 20 to 30 minutes until chicken is at 165°F and cheese is fully melted. Remove from the oven.

Once plated, top with extra French onion soup from the skillet. Serve and enjoy!

Clean-Out-Your-Fridge Balsamic Chicken Bake

Yield: 2 servings

Gluten-free | Low-fat | Nut-free
Option: Dairy-free | Lower-carb

What you'll need:

3 cups gluten-free chicken tenders (page 126)

1½–2 cups light balsamic vinaigrette dressing

Mix-Ins:

1 bag fresh spinach

1 large eggplant, cut into 1-inch cubes

1 cup roasted red peppers, jarred

½ cup roasted banana peppers, jarred

½ cup sun-dried tomatoes, jarred

Dairy-free option: Make sure the light balsamic vinaigrette dressing is dairy-free

Lower-carb option: Since the chicken is breaded, this won't be a low-carb meal, but using different rice can still make this a lower carb meal.*

How to Make This Lower Carb*

For a healthier option, use brown rice. But for a lower-carb option, use half brown rice and half vegetable rice, like cauliflower rice. Feel free to use lentil rice, riced broccoli, or riced butternut squash. If you choose to use all vegetable rice, the rice will be lower in carbs, but you will get a softer textured base. I always recommend adding some brown or white rice to the vegetable rice for a better texture.

This one I learned from my mother-in-law! It's a total "clean out your fridge" recipe, meaning any jarred or fresh vegetables you have you can throw in here! Feel free to do more of an Italian flair with roasted red peppers, roasted tomatoes, and eggplant, or you can do a heavier vegetable combination with spinach, onions, and mushrooms. This recipe can be hearty and served with white rice or lentil pasta, or lean and served with cauliflower rice or brown rice. This recipe uses no oil and no butter to keep this meal lean and low in saturated fat!

What to do:

Preheat the oven to 350°F. Place chicken pieces in a 9 × 12–inch baking dish. Add mix-in vegetables. Pour balsamic vinaigrette over top. Bake uncovered for 30 to 45 minutes.

This bake is best served over rice or with gluten-free pasta. Or use any rice you want! Choose from brown rice or white rice. The rice gives the meal a hearty texture and carries the sauce well.

Fresh or jarred vegetables?
This recipe can also be considered a clean-out-your-pantry type of recipe. You can use any pickled or jarred vegetable you want, including jarred tomatoes, sun-dried tomatoes, mushrooms, fresh spinach pickled onions, giardiniera, artichoke hearts, etc.

One-Pan Chicken Sausage and Rice Casserole

Yield: 4 servings

Gluten-free | Dairy-free | Nut-free
Option: Lower-carb | Vegan

What you'll need:

6 links sweet, fully-cooked Italian chicken sauces

3 cups instant or frozen brown or white rice, fully cooked

1½ cups cauliflower rice (or sub other riced vegetable)

2 cups diced bell peppers

½ cup diced red onions

1 cup crushed tomatoes or diced tomatoes

2 tablespoons vegan butter

1 tablespoon minced garlic

½ cup vegetable broth

¼ cup vegan/dairy-free parmesan cheese

½ teaspoon salt

½ teaspoon pepper

Lower-carb option: Use half brown rice instead of white rice. If you need an even lower-carb option, choose to use all vegetable rice and no brown rice! The recipe will be very low in carbs, but you will get a softer casserole texture. I recommend using brown rice and cauliflower rice together.

Vegan option: Use vegan sausage

This cozy Italian casserole is a perfect quick casserole for an easy weeknight meal. To save time, the casserole uses fully cooked rice—and chicken sausages that come fully cooked already! Casseroles with raw meat and uncooked rice can sometimes take all day to cook, but this casserole only takes 20 to 30 minutes!

What to do:

Preheat the oven to 400°F. Cut the chicken sausages into 1-inch slices. Add chicken sausage slices, rice, cauliflower rice, peppers, onions, tomatoes, butter, and minced garlic into a 9 × 12–inch baking dish. Mix together and make a smooth, even layer. Pour vegetable broth over top. Sprinkle parmesan cheese, salt, and pepper on top.

Bake uncovered for 20 to 30 minutes. All liquid should be absorbed, and rice should be soft and fluffy in the center but crispy and browned along the edges.

Save Some Time

This recipe calls for fully cooked rice to cut down on bake time. Use leftover rice that you've already made or instant microwavable rice or frozen rice.

Easy Taco Lasagna

Yield: 3-4 servings

Gluten-free | Nut-free
Options: Dairy-free | Lower-carb | Low-fat | Vegan

What you'll need:

2 cups taco sauce or salsa

6-9 corn tortillas

2 cups cauliflower rice (or sub other vegetable rice)

2 cups instant or frozen brown or white rice, fully cooked

1 bell pepper, diced

½ cup diced tomatoes

½ cup diced red onion

2 cups shredded chicken or shredded jackfruit

½ cup cheddar cheese

For your topping:

Vegan Avocado Crema (page 24)

Fresh arugula

Dairy-free option: Use vegan/dairy-free cheese

Lower-carb option: Use half brown rice instead of white rice. If you need an even lower-carb option, choose to use all vegetable rice and no brown rice! The recipe will be very low in carbs, but you will get a softer casserole texture. I recommend using brown rice and cauliflower rice together.

Low-fat option: Use fat-free cheese

Vegan option: Use vegan/dairy-free cheese and shredded jackfruit

I love a cozy casserole. Especially in the week. They taste like they've been baking all day and are packed with flavor, but they are actually saving you loads of time! This easy taco lasagna is a casserole filled with taco flavoring, but with corn tortillas layered like lasagna noodles. This Easy Taco Lasagna takes 5 minutes to throw together and is packed with peppers, onions, tomatoes, cheddar, and taco seasoning.

What to do:

Preheat the oven to 425°F. In a baking dish, add 2 tablespoons taco sauce to the bottom of the dish to keep the tortillas from sticking. Cover the bottom of the baking dish with the corn tortillas. Some will have to be cut in half to cover all the edges and corners.

Top with an even layer of cauliflower rice and brown rice. Next, create another layer of corn tortillas. Top this layer evenly with peppers, tomatoes, onions, and chicken. Next, create a top layer with corn tortillas. Cover this tortilla layer with cheese. Bake for 20 to 30 minutes, remove foil, and cook an additional 10 minutes to brown the cheese on top.

All ingredients are already cooked before being added to the casserole, so the baking is just to warm the ingredients and let them blend together. The top layer of cheese should be melted and browned. The corn tortillas should be crispy along the outside edges.

Save Some Time

If you want to prepare this meal ahead of time, dice up the vegetables in advance and make the shredded chicken in advance. Store them in an airtight container in the fridge for up to 3 days.

To prepare the chicken in advance, I put 2 boneless breasts of chicken in the crockpot with 1 cup of water. Water should fully cover chicken. Cook on high for 1 to 2 hours. Remove chicken. Chicken should be easily shredded with two forks. If you cannot break the chicken apart easily, it will need more time to cook. Season with salt and pepper.

Instead of making chicken at home and shredding it, buy a rotisserie chicken from the grocery store and easily shred the chicken yourself. Note that a warm rotisserie chicken is easier to shred than a refrigerated one, so I prefer to shred the rotisserie chicken as soon as I get home. Store the shredded chicken in an airtight container for 1 to 3 days in the refrigerator until you are ready to use it.

For a Spicier Option

Drizzle hot sauce on the top before baking or top your individual portion with hot sauce if only one person wants a spicy option!

Chicken and Peas Casserole

Yield: 3 servings

Gluten-free | Nut-free
Options: Dairy-free | Low-fat

What you'll need:

½ cup uncooked white or brown rice

2 cups frozen peas

8 ounces chicken stock

1 teaspoon salt

1 teaspoon pepper

½ cup parmesan cheese

2 tablespoons vegan butter

2 eggs

2 cups gluten-free breadcrumbs

2 (6-ounce) chicken breasts

Dairy-free option: Use vegan/dairy-free grated parmesan cheese

Low-fat option: Use fat-free grated parmesan cheese. Dip chicken into egg whites instead of full eggs.

I've been making this chicken and pea casserole since I was in college! It's easy, healthy, and a great meal-prep option. I would make a big tray of it on Sunday night and eat it for dinner for the next three or four nights. This chicken and peas casserole has crispy breaded chicken breasts and is loaded with peas. The rice is fluffy in the middle and gets crispy around the edges. Then to seal the deal, this casserole is topped with Parmesan!

What to do:

Preheat the oven to 400°F. In a 9 × 12–inch oven-safe dish, add rice and peas. Pour chicken stock over the rice and peas. Top with salt, pepper, parmesan cheese, and sections of vegan butter evenly distributed.

Crack 2 eggs into a separate bowl. Scramble and set aside.

Pour gluten-free breadcrumbs into a separate bowl. Set aside.

Dip first chicken breast into the egg mixture, then the breadcrumbs. Fully cover chicken with breadcrumbs, pressing the crumbs in to make sure they stick. Place chicken breast in the baking dish and repeat the process with the second chicken breast. Cover with aluminum foil and add to the oven. Bake for 30 minutes. Remove aluminum foil and bake for another 10 to 20 minutes, until chicken is fully cooked.

Check the interior temperature of chicken to make sure it is fully cooked at 165°F. All chicken stock should be absorbed. Rice should be soft and cooked. Rice will be crispy along the casserole edges. Remove from the oven and serve!

Andrew's Weeknight Turkey Chili

Yield: 4–6 servings

Gluten-free | Dairy-free | Low-fat | Nut-free

What you'll need:

1 large bell pepper

1 large onion

2 tablespoons olive oil

1 pound lean ground turkey

1 (15-ounce) can beans of choice (we use kidney beans!)

2 (15-ounce) cans tomato sauce

1 (15-ounce) can diced or crushed tomatoes

3 tablespoons chili powder

2 teaspoons cumin

1 teaspoon paprika

1 tablespoon garlic powder

1 teaspoon red pepper flakes

½ teaspoon cayenne pepper

½ teaspoon salt

½ teaspoon pepper

2 tablespoons brown sugar, coconut sugar, or sugar substitute

Andrew, my fiancé, loves to make chili. It could be a 90°F afternoon in the middle of August, and he'll be in the kitchen dicing the peppers and onions and preparing the chili. I'm telling you, any day of the week, any month of the year, he's down for chili. I, on the other hand, love chili only on a crisp, fall Sunday while watching football. But, whether you're like him or like me, his turkey chili recipe is loaded with flavors that tastes like it has been cooking all day, but . . . this easy chili really only takes 20 minutes to prep and then simmers on the stove for 1 to 2 hours.

What to do:

On a cutting board, dice up the pepper and onion. In a large pot, add the olive oil, peppers, onions, and ground turkey. Cook for 5 to 7 minutes on medium heat until the peppers and onions are soft and meat is browned.

In the same pot, add in the beans, tomato sauce, crushed tomatoes, chili powder, cumin, paprika, garlic powder, red pepper flakes, cayenne pepper, salt, pepper, and sugar.

Cook covered, on medium-low heat, for 1 to 2 hours. Stir every 15 to 20 minutes. When chili is done cooking, remove from the stove and ladle 1 to 2 cups into individual serving bowls.

Optional toppings

I like to serve this chili over rice! You can choose from ½ cup fully cooked white or ½ cup fully cooked brown rice or, for a lower-carb option, use ¼ cup brown rice mixed with ¼ cup cauliflower rice. Top individual portions with fat free cheddar cheese or dairy-free cheddar cheese. Add slices of avocado on top. Add crispy corn tortilla strips on top, too.

Korean-Style Ground Turkey and Green Beans, page 148

It's Not Take-Out, It's Fake-Out

When I first went gluten-free, I had a complete breakdown about never getting to eat easy take-out food again. I loved pizza on Friday nights, easy Chinese food, and ordering all of it without a second thought. Now, *everything* was a second thought. Does the Chinese food have soy sauce in it? Yes. So that wasn't safe to order. Did the pizza place have gluten-free crusts? That gave me anxiety. Did the gluten-free crusts they had have almonds in it? It was dizzying. But slowly, I began the process of re-creating my favorite takeout, at home in my own kitchen.

I could use my own gluten-free crust, I could use a dairy-free cheese, and I could still create the same flavors and the same feelings of the takeout I was used to. Making take-out dishes at home quickly became one of my favorite things to do, and even now, I find myself always keeping Chinese ingredients and gluten-free pizza crusts in the pantry so I can make the fake-out take-out on a Saturday night any time I want to.

Korean-Style Ground Turkey and Green Beans

Yield: 1½ cups ground turkey and vegetable mixture with ½ cup rice (serves 2)

Gluten-free | Dairy-free
Options: Lower-carb | Nut-free | Vegan | Vegetarian

For your ground turkey:

1 pound ground turkey

1 teaspoon salt

1 teaspoon pepper

1 tablespoon sesame oil

1 tablespoon minced garlic

2 teaspoons ground ginger

For your veggies:

2 cups green beans, sliced red bell peppers, sliced white onions, or broccoli florets

1 teaspoon oil of choice or light cooking spray

For your sauce:

¼ cup gluten-free soy sauce or coconut aminos

2 teaspoons cornstarch

1½ tablespoon brown sugar, coconut sugar, or sugar substitute

a pinch of red chili flakes, optional

For your topping:

2 teaspoons sesame seeds

2 tablespoons cashews, optional

For your carb or grain:*

1 cup fully cooked white OR

1 cup fully cooked sticky rice OR

1 cup fully cooked brown rice OR

½ cup brown rice mixed with ½ cup cauliflower rice

Lower-carb option: Serve over brown rice + cauliflower rice mixed

Nut-free option: Nix the cashews! You can replace them with crispy chickpeas if you need a good crunch.

Vegan option: Eliminate the ground turkey and add 2 extra cups of vegetables. Make sure the sugar you have is vegan-friendly or use coconut sugar.

Vegetarian option: Eliminate the ground turkey and add 2 extra cups of vegetables

This thirty-minute Korean-style turkey and green beans is a perfect weeknight meal packed with flavor! Basically it's what I would ideally order for a Friday night take-out meal, but with a healthy twist! This recipe uses ground turkey instead of ground beef, and a minimal amount of oil, to make it a perfect healthy "fake-out" meal!

What to do:

Make the ground turkey

In a frying pan, sauté ground turkey in a pan with salt, pepper, sesame oil, minced garlic, and ground ginger. Allow turkey to reach the appropriate temperature to be fully cooked, at least 165°F. Ground turkey should be browned and not pink in the center.

---

* See Part 2: Gluten-free/Nut-free bread and grain substitutes: Gluten-free grains and rice for more info on selecting rice and cooking it; see Part 5: Low-carb substitutes for how to sub cauliflower rice for a lower-carb option.

Make the vegetables

In a separate pan, sauté choice of vegetables until fully cooked. You can add cooking spray or 1 teaspoon of oil of choice to keep vegetables from sticking or burning.

Make the sauce

In a separate bowl, mix together ingredients for the Korean-style sauce. Add to saucepan and simmer on low heat for 3 to 5 minutes until sauce thickens up. Sauce should be thick, not water-like thin.

Put everything together

Once turkey is fully cooked and vegetables are cooked and soft, combine in one pan and pour sauce over top. Let vegetables and meat warm with sauce for 3 to 5 minutes.

This dish is best served over fully cooked rice: brown rice, white rice, sticky rice, vegetable rice, or a combination. Vegetable or cauliflower rice will be the lowest carb option. Feel free to use instant rice, frozen rice, or make your own! Top with sesame seeds and option to add cashews on top for flavor and crunch.

Healthier-Than-Takeout Orange Chicken and Rice

Yield: 2 meals

Gluten-free | Dairy-free | Nut-free
Options: Vegan/vegetarian

For your orange sauce:

¾ cup orange marmalade

¼ cup gluten-free soy sauce, coconut aminos, or liquid aminos

3 tablespoons rice wine vinegar

1 tablespoon cornstarch

2 teaspoons minced garlic

½ tablespoon ground ginger

½ cup of water

For your carb or grain:*

1 cup fully cooked white OR

1 cup fully cooked sticky rice OR

1 cup fully cooked brown rice OR

½ cup brown rice mixed with ½ cup cauliflower rice

What else you'll need:

2 cups broccoli

1 teaspoon olive oil or oil of choice

1 tablespoon minced garlic

crispy cauliflower, optional

For your potential protein:

½ pound chicken breasts, cut into 1-inch cubes

1 teaspoon olive oil or oil of choice

Vegan/vegetarian option: Add crispy cauliflower instead of grilled chicken

Like I said, when I first went gluten free, I had a complete breakdown about never getting to eat Chinese food again. But a few years ago, I finally got the courage to make my own, and I immediately wondered what I had been so scared of! "At-home takeout" quickly became one of my favorite things to make.

What to do:

In a medium-sized bowl, mix together the orange sauce ingredients. Add sauce to a pot or pan and warm on medium heat until the sauce starts to thicken. While the sauce is warming, chop up broccoli and add to a separate frying pan with 1 teaspoon oil and 1 teaspoon minced garlic. Sauté for 5 to 8 minutes until broccoli is soft. If desired, add chicken or crispy cauliflower.

To add chicken, add to the frying pan with 1 teaspoon oil and sauté until the chicken is fully cooked. Check temperature with a meat thermometer. Center should not be pink; chicken should be 165°F.

To serve, separate the rice into 2 equal portions. Plate the rice, top each plate with broccoli and chicken and/or cauliflower. Top with sauce. Serve and enjoy.

---

* See Part 2: Gluten-free/nut-free bread and grain substitutes: Gluten-free grains and rice for more info on selecting rice and cooking it; see Part 5: Low-carb substitutes for how to sub cauliflower rice for a lower-carb option.

Spicy Pepperoni and Hot Honey Pizza

Yield: 1 individual pizza

Gluten-free | Nut-free
Options: Dairy-free | Low-fat | Lower-carb | Vegan

What you'll need:

1 gluten-free pizza crust (page 15)

For your toppings:

½–1 cup tomato or marinara sauce

2 cups mozzarella

¼ cup chicken sausage

¼ cup turkey pepperoni

¼ cup banana peppers, jarred and diced

¼ cup roasted red peppers, jarred and diced

2 tablespoons red onion

2 tablespoons hot honey

Dairy-free option: Use vegan/dairy-free cheese. Make sure marinara sauce is dairy-free.

Low-fat option: Use fat-free cheese. Use turkey pepperoni and chicken sausage instead of pork or beef.

Lower-carb option: Use cauliflower crust

Vegan option: Use vegan/dairy-free cheese as well as vegan pepperoni/sausage. Make sure marinara sauce is vegan. Use vegan honey + red pepper flakes instead of hot honey.

This pizza is a favorite in my household! When I was a kid, we used to get these personal frozen pizzas, 10 for $10. They only had a few toppings but supreme was one of them! They were saved for special days, like first lunches of the summer or Saturday nights at home. I loved them! This pizza is a spicy supreme-like pizza topped with healthier versions of the same toppings I used to get as a kid. It uses dairy-free cheese instead of dairy cheese, turkey pepperoni instead of regular beef or pork pepperoni, and chicken sausage as a leaner option.

What to do:

Preheat oven to 400°F. Prepare crust of choice. Prebake crust until crispy.

Remove crust from oven and top with tomato sauce, mozzarella, sliced sausage, pepperoni, banana peppers, roasted red peppers, and diced red onion. I like the add pools of tomato sauce instead of spreading sauce over the whole pizza.

Add crust back to oven and bake until cheese is melted, toppings are warm, and edges of crust are crispy and brown. Cook time will vary depending on the crust you choose. Remove from oven. Top with drizzle of hot honey. Slice and serve!

Healthy Lettuce Wraps
with an Easy Peanut Sauce

Yield: 2–3 servings

Gluten-free | Dairy-free | Low-carb
Options: Nut-free | Vegan/vegetarian

For the peanut sauce:

½ cup peanut butter

⅓ cup water

4 tablespoons coconut aminos (or liquid aminos or gluten-free soy sauce)

2 tablespoons rice vinegar

1 tablespoon sugar-free maple syrup, honey, or agave

½ tablespoon sesame oil

½ teaspoon ground ginger

½ teaspoon garlic powder

For your base sauce:

1 cup water

¼ cup coconut aminos (or liquid aminos or gluten-free soy sauce)

1 tablespoon rice vinegar

2 tablespoons cornstarch

½ teaspoon powdered ginger

½ teaspoon powdered garlic

1 teaspoon sriracha, optional

What else you'll need:

2 bell peppers

½ white onion

light cooking spray

salt, optional

pepper, optional

1 full head leafy greens such as butter lettuce, bibb lettuce, or romaine lettuce

½ cup cashews (omit for nut allergy)

For your potential protein:

1 pound ground turkey or ground chicken

Nut-free option: Nix the cashews! You can replace them with crispy chickpeas if you need a good crunch. Swap tahini or nut-free spread instead of peanut butter! It will change the flavor profile, but the texture will stay the same.

Vegan/vegetarian option: Eliminate the ground turkey and add 2 extra cups of vegetables

Lettuce wraps are a fun play on a low-carb meal. These are topped with peppers, onions, and a spicy peanut sauce. They are low carb since there is no rice or grain involved—only vegetables, sauces, and potential protein!

What to do:

Make the peanut sauce

In a medium-sized bowl, mix together the peanut sauce and set aside.

Make the base sauce

In a separate bowl, mix together the base sauce ingredients and add to a saucepan, cooking on medium-low heat to let the sauce slowly thicken.

Prepare the vegetables

On a cutting board, dice peppers and onion into small, fine pieces. Pieces should be no bigger than your fingernail. In a separate pan, sauté the peppers and onions until fully soft. Add light oil spray, if needed. Set aside.

Prepare your protein
In the same pan, add the ground meat. If you need to use light oil spray, you can add that now. You can add salt and pepper now, too. If you are adding cashews, mix them in here. Cook on medium heat until ground meat has reached a safe temperature of 165°F. (Eliminate this step if choosing the vegan/vegetarian option.)

Once the ground meat (optional), peppers, and onions are fully cooked, add the base sauce only and let simmer for 3 to 4 minutes until it has thickened. Remove from stove top and add to the serving bowl.

Serve the bowl of peppers, onions, and ground turkey. Serve the peanut sauce separately. Serve cashews separately for topping. Place your green leaves onto a plate and add to the table to allow everyone to make their own lettuce wraps as you eat.

I like to make each lettuce wrap as I eat them, but you can top all the lettuce pieces ahead of time if you want. Use individual pieces of lettuce as a taco-like shell and top with meat, peppers, and onions. Layer the peppers, onions, meat, and cashew mixture onto the leaf, and top with peanut sauce. Feel free to double up the leaf for extra support so the lettuce wrap does not rip or tear when eating. If desired, add sesame seeds, avocado, or rice.

Skinny Buffalo Chicken Pizza

Yield: 1 individual pizza

Gluten-free | Nut-free
Options: Dairy-free | Low-fat | Lower-carb | Vegan

What you'll need:

1 gluten-free pizza crust (page 15)

For your toppings:

1 (6-ounce) grilled chicken breast or chicken cutlet

2 tablespoons Two-Ingredient Spicy Buffalo Sauce (page 33)

½ cup mozzarella cheese

½ cup cheddar cheese

2 handfuls arugula

2 tablespoons diced red onion

2 tablespoons diced tomatoes

¼ avocado, cut into ½-inch cubes

2 tablespoons chopped scallions

2 tablespoons ranch

Dairy-free option: Use vegan/dairy-free cheese and ranch

Low-fat option: Use fat-free cheese, fat-free ranch, and grilled chicken

Lower-carb option: Use cauliflower crust and grilled chicken

Vegan option: Use vegan chick'n substitute and vegan/dairy-free cheese

When I was in college, after a night out, my friends and I would always grab a slice of buffalo chicken pizza on our way home. Did it make it feel good? Emotionally, yes. I loved it. Did it make me feel good physically? No way. I had a raging stomachache all night. It was packed with gluten and dairy and probably a million other preservatives and ingredients and oils I didn't realize I was eating. So now, I make this healthier, gluten-free, dairy-free version at home that makes me feel just as happy, but without the stomachache.

What to do:

Preheat oven to 400°F. Prepare crust of choice. Prebake crust until crispy.

On a cutting board, cut up the grilled chicken into ½-inch cubes. Chicken should be fully cooked ahead of time. Add chicken to a separate bowl and mix with 2 tablespoons of buffalo sauce. Top crust with cheese and diced chicken.

Add crust back to oven and bake until cheese is melted, toppings are warm, and edges of crust are crispy and brown. Cook time will vary depending on the crust you choose.

Once the pizza is finished baking, remove from oven and top with arugula, red onions, tomato, avocado, and scallions. Drizzle ranch. Slice into 4 or 6 pieces and serve.

Butternut Squash and Roasted Garlic Pizza

Yield: 1 individual pizza

Gluten-free | Nut-free | Vegetarian
Options: Dairy-free | Low-fat | Lower-carb | Vegan

What you'll need:

1 gluten-free pizza crust (page 15)

For your toppings:

2 garlic cloves

2 tablespoons olive oil, divided

1 cup ½-inch butternut squash cubes

¼ cup thinly sliced onions

1 teaspoon cinnamon

1 teaspoon cayenne pepper

1 cup fresh spinach

1 cup goat cheese

1 cup cheddar cheese

1 cup mozzarella cheese

1 teaspoon garlic powder

1 tablespoon maple syrup, honey, or agave

2 tablespoons pumpkin seeds or pepitas

salt and pepper, to taste

Dairy-free option: Use all vegan/dairy-free cheeses

Low-fat option: Use fat-free cheeses. Sub fat-free feta for goat cheese. Eliminate the olive oil drizzle.

Lower-carb option: Use cauliflower crust

Vegan option: Use all vegan/dairy-free cheeses and sugar-free maple syrup or agave. Skip the honey.

This pizza is perfect for a crisp fall night. It's packed with in-season produce and fall flavors then drizzled with honey and olive oil. It's perfect for a fall dinner outside, paired with some wine, a warm blanket, and some candles.

What to do:

Preheat oven to 400°F. Prepare crust of choice. Prebake crust until crispy.

Next, peel garlic and add cloves to aluminum foil. Top with 1 tablespoon olive oil. Wrap garlic and olive oil into a ball and bake for 30 minutes. When it is done, garlic should be soft and easy mashed with a fork. Set aside.

While crust is baking, add the butternut squash cubes to a frying pan with 1 tablespoon olive oil, onions, cinnamon, cayenne pepper, and fresh spinach. Sauté on medium heat for approximately 10 minutes until the butternut squash cubes are browned along the edges and the onions are translucent and caramelized.

Remove crust from oven and add small pools of mashed garlic and small pools of goat cheese. Then top with mozzarella, cheddar, butternut squash, spinach, and onions. Drizzle with honey. Add crust back to oven and bake until cheese is melted, toppings are warm, and edges of crust are crispy and brown. Cook time will vary depending on the crust you choose.

Remove from oven. Top with pumpkin seeds, olive oil, salt, and pepper. Slice into 4 or 6 pieces and serve.

White Pizza
with Zucchini and Balsamic Glaze

Yield: 1 individual pizza

Gluten-free | Nut-free | Vegetarian
Options: Dairy-free | Low-fat | Lower-carb | Vegan

What you'll need:

1 gluten-free pizza crust (page 15)

For your toppings:

1 zucchini

2 cups mozzarella

½ cup ricotta

1 cup arugula

1 tablespoon balsamic glaze

Dairy-free option: Use vegan/dairy-free cheeses

Low-fat option: Use fat-free cheeses

Lower-carb option: Use cauliflower crust

Vegan option: Use vegan/dairy-free cheeses

Sometimes I'm just not a huge fan of tomato sauce or marinara sauce. I basically just want cheesy bread, and that, by its more formal name, is just white pizza. White pizza is packed with mozzarella and ricotta but a tad bit healthier than what you'd get at a traditional pizza shop. And while that version is hands-down fantastic, this healthier version promises less of a stomachache.

What to do:

Preheat oven to 400°F. Prepare crust of choice. Prebake crust until crispy.

On a cutting board, slice the zucchini into thin ribbons. The zucchini ribbons should be so thin you can almost see through it. This way, you can allow the zucchini to bake while the pizza is baking and not have to go through the extra step of cooking to zucchini separately.

Remove crust from oven and top with mozzarella, ricotta, and zucchini slices. Add crust back to oven and bake until cheese is melted, toppings are warm, and edges of crust are crispy and brown. Cook time will vary depending on the crust you choose.

Remove from oven. Top with arugula and drizzle with balsamic glaze. Slice into 4 or 6 pieces and serve.

Cacio e Pepe Pizza

Yield: 1 individual pizza

Gluten-free | Nut-free | Vegetarian
Options: Dairy-free | Low-fat | Lower-carb | Vegan

What you'll need:

1 gluten-free pizza crust (page 15)

For your toppings:

2 cups mozzarella

½ cup ricotta

3 garlic cloves

2 tablespoons olive oil, divided

2 teaspoons cracked pepper

3 tablespoons grated parmesan cheese

Dairy-free option: Use vegan/dairy-free cheeses

Low-fat option: Use fat-free cheeses

Lower-carb option: Use cauliflower crust

Vegan option: Use vegan/dairy-free cheeses

Anyone who can pass up a cacio e pepe pasta dish on a menu deserves some extra points from me. Because I, as well as many of you, I assume, cannot pass up that dish. I developed this pizza one Friday night when I was really craving the pasta version but also wanted some crispy crust. It's all the great flavors of cacio e pepe pasta but could be a healthier, dairy-free version on a gluten-free crust.

What to do:

Preheat oven to 400°F. Peel garlic and add cloves to aluminum foil. Top with 1 tablespoon olive oil. Wrap garlic and olive oil into a ball and bake for 30 minutes. Remove roasted garlic. After baking, garlic should be soft and easily spreadable.

Prepare crust of choice. Prebake crust until crispy.

Remove crust from oven and top with mozzarella and scattered pools of ricotta. Add spreadable garlic onto pizza crust in scattered areas. Garlic doesn't need to be spread on the entire pizza. Top with cracked pepper and parmesan cheese. Drizzle pizza with remaining olive oil.

Add crust back to oven and bake until cheese is melted, toppings are warm, and edges of crust are crispy and brown. Cook time will vary depending on the crust you choose. Remove from oven. Slice into 4 or 6 pieces and serve.

Prosciutto, Arugula, and Fig Pizza

Yield: 1 individual pizza

Gluten-free | Nut-free
Options: Dairy-free | Low-fat | Lower-carb | Vegan

What you'll need:

1 gluten-free pizza crust (page 15)

For your toppings:

3 garlic cloves

1 tablespoon olive oil

1 cup mozzarella

½ cup garlic and herb brie cheese

salt and pepper, to taste

1 cup arugula

1 tablespoon balsamic glaze

3–5 slices prosciutto

3 figs

Dairy-free option: Use vegan/dairy-free cheeses

Low-fat option: Use fat-free cheeses

Lower-carb option: Use cauliflower crust

Vegan option: Use vegan/dairy-free cheeses. Ditch the prosciutto.

Sweet and salty pizzas are always a crowd-pleaser! This prosciutto, arugula, and fig pizza has the salty prosciutto and the sweet figs and those flavors are married together with a creamy garlic and herb brie cheese. This pizza is perfect for a fall date night at home or cut into 2-inch squares to be a fun party snack or a flavorful appetizer!

What to do:

Preheat oven to 400°F. Peel garlic and add cloves to aluminum foil. Top with 1 tablespoon olive oil. Wrap garlic and olive oil into a ball and bake for 30 minutes. Remove roasted garlic. After baking, garlic should be soft and easily spreadable.

Prepare crust of choice. Prebake crust until crispy. Remove crust from oven and top with garlic, mozzarella, and brie. Add spreadable garlic onto pizza crust in scattered areas. Garlic doesn't need to be spread on the entire pizza. Top with salt and pepper.

Add crust back to oven and bake until cheese is melted, toppings are warm, and edges of crust are crispy and brown. Cook time will vary depending on the crust you choose. Remove pizza from oven, top with arugula, balsamic glaze, prosciutto, and figs. Slice into 4 or 6 pieces and serve.

Caramelized Onions and Pear Pizza

Yield: 1 individual pizza

Gluten-free | Nut-free | Vegetarian
Options: Dairy-free | Low-fat | Lower-carb | Vegan

What you'll need:

1 gluten-free pizza crust (page 15)

For your toppings:

2 cups herb-infused cheddar

2 tablespoons roasted garlic

1 + ½ tablespoon olive oil

salt and pepper, to taste

1 pear

1 small onion

1 cup arugula

1 tablespoon white balsamic glaze

Dairy-free option: Use vegan/dairy-free cheese

Low-fat option: Use fat-free cheese

Lower-carb option: Use cauliflower crust

Vegan option: Use vegan/dairy-free cheese

Pizzas made with cheeses other than mozzarella hold a special place in my heart. I especially love melted cheddar on a pizza. When the edges get browned and the cheddar gets crispy, it's life changing. This cheddar pizza is topped with thinly sliced and roasted pears, caramelized onions, and loaded with fresh arugula and a white balsamic drizzle. It's perfect for an at-home pizza night or for serving mini slices as a crowd-pleasing appetizer.

What to do:

Preheat oven to 400°F. Peel garlic and add cloves to aluminum foil. Top with 1 tablespoon olive oil. Wrap garlic and olive oil into a ball and bake for 30 minutes. Remove roasted garlic. After baking, garlic should be soft and easily spreadable.

Prepare crust of choice. Prebake crust until crispy.

On a cutting board, slice onion and pears into thin slices. Slices should be as thin as possible, almost able to see through. In a frying pan, add ½ tablespoon olive oil, pears, and onions. Sauté on low heat for 10 to 15 minutes until onions are caramelized and pears are soft and roasted. Pears should be slightly browned on the edges. Remove from heat and set aside.

Remove crust from oven and top with garlic. Add spreadable garlic onto pizza crust in scattered areas. Garlic doesn't need to be spread on the entire pizza. Next, add cheese, onions, pears, salt, and pepper.

Add crust back to oven and bake until cheese is melted, toppings are warm, and edges of crust are crispy and brown. Cook time will vary depending on the crust you choose. Remove pizza from oven; top with arugula and drizzle with balsamic glaze. Slice into 4 or 6 pieces and serve.

White Pizza with Pesto Aioli (front) and Spicy Pepperoni and Hot Honey Pizza, pages 167 and 151

White Pizza
with Pesto Aioli

Yield: 1 individual pizza

Gluten-free | Nut-free | Vegetarian
Options: Dairy-free | Low-fat | Lower-carb | Vegan

What you'll need:
1 gluten-free pizza crust (page 15)

For your toppings:
2–3 tablespoons Arugula Pesto Aioli (page 25)
2 cups mozzarella
¼ cup shredded parmesan
2 tablespoons diced red onion
¼ cup diced tomatoes
¼ cup arugula

Dairy-free option: Use vegan/dairy-free cheese
Low-fat option: Use fat-free cheeses
Lower-carb option: Use cauliflower crust
Vegan option: Use vegan/dairy-free cheeses

What to do:
Preheat oven to 400°F. Prepare crust of choice. Prebake crust until crispy.

Remove crust from oven and top with pools of arugula pesto aioli, mozzarella, and parmesan. I like the add pools of pesto instead of spreading the pesto over the whole pizza.

Add crust back to oven and bake until cheese is melted, toppings are warm, and edges of crust are crispy and brown. Cook time will vary depending on the crust you choose.

Remove from oven. Top with red onion, tomatoes, and arugula. Slice and serve!

Easy BBQ Chicken Pizza

Yield: 1 individual pizza

Gluten-free | Nut-free
Options: Dairy-free | Low-fat | Lower-carb | Lower-sugar | Vegan

What you'll need:

1 gluten-free pizza crust (page 15)

For your toppings:

¼ cup onions

1 cup cheddar cheese

1 cup mozzarella

1 cup shredded grilled chicken

¼ cup BBQ sauce

2 tablespoons ranch

Dairy-free option: Use vegan/dairy-free cheeses and dairy-free ranch

Low-fat option: Use fat-free cheeses and ranch

Lower-carb options: Use cauliflower crust

Lower-sugar option: Use sugar-free BBQ sauce

Vegan option: Use vegan/dairy-free cheese, vegan chick'n substitute, jackfruit, and vegan ranch

What to do:

Preheat oven to 400°F. Prepare crust of choice. Prebake crust until crispy.

On a cutting board, slice onion into thin slices. Slices should be as thin as possible, almost able to see through.

Remove crust from oven and top with cheddar, mozzarella, shredded chicken or jackfruit and onions.

Add crust back to oven and bake until cheese is melted, toppings are warm, and edges of crust are crispy and brown. Cook time will vary depending on the crust you choose.

Remove from oven. Top with drizzle of BBQ sauce and ranch. Slice and serve!

Beet, Goat Cheese, and Caramelized Onion Pizza

Yield: 1 individual pizza

Gluten-free | Vegetarian
Options: Dairy-free | Low-fat | Lower-carb | Nut-free | Vegan

What you'll need:

1 gluten-free pizza crust (page 15)

For your toppings:

1 cup mozzarella

¼ cup goat cheese or cream cheese

¼ cup onions

½ tablespoon olive oil or oil of choice

⅓ cup beets, roasted and diced

1 cup arugula

1 tablespoon balsamic glaze

salt and pepper, to taste

2 tablespoons candied pecans

Dairy-free option: Use vegan/dairy-free cheeses

Low-fat option: Use fat-free cheeses, sub fat-free feta for goat cheese

Lower-carb option: Use cauliflower crust

Nut-free option: Use cinnamon-sugar crispy chickpeas instead of pecans

Vegan option: Use vegan/dairy-free cheeses

For my mom's birthday every year, we make pizzas at home. We started by choosing recipes from a cookbook, and then each year, we'd adjust or make changes and substitute and the recipes grew along with myself and my family over the years. This beet and goat cheese one is one I've been making for a few years and is a fun take on a traditional beet and goat cheese salad. This pizza is packed with the same flavors as one of my favorite salads, just on a crispy pizza crust! There's something about adding fresh arugula to a pizza that makes it feel automatically healthy!

What to do:

Preheat oven to 400°F. Prepare crust of choice. Prebake crust until crispy.

Remove crust from oven and top with pools of goat cheese. Cover the remaining crust with mozzarella.

On a cutting board, slice onion into thin slices. Slices should be as thin as possible, almost able to see through. In a frying pan, add olive oil and onions. Sauté on low heat for 15 to 20 minutes until onions are caramelized.

Add crust back to oven and bake until cheese is melted, toppings are warm, and edges of crust are crispy and brown. Cook time will vary depending on the crust you choose.

Remove from oven. Top with caramelized onions, diced beets, arugula, balsamic glaze, salt and pepper, and candied pecans. Slice and serve!

Chocolate Chip Pancake Bread, page 191

Healthier Desserts and Treats

Do you ever walk into a bakery and want everything? But then you see the sign that says "If you're allergic to nuts, please don't order here" and that doesn't make you feel very good. Or maybe you look at all those treats and immediately think about the saturated fat in it because you have high cholesterol, or you think about the sugar content in it because you're diabetic. Whatever your dietary need or preference is, you shouldn't have to give up all desserts. There are desserts for you. They may not be in a fancy bakeshop, or at your corner bakery, but there are recipes out there for delicious desserts that are lower in fat, lower in sugar, vegan, gluten-free, or dairy-free that you'll be making over and over again.

Mini Chocolate Chip Pumpkin Breads

Yield: 6–8 mini loaves

Gluten-free | Low-fat | Nut-free
Options: Dairy-free | Lower-sugar | Vegan

For your base:

1 mashed banana

1 cup applesauce

½ cup pumpkin puree

½ cup maple syrup, honey, or agave

⅓ cup plant-based milk

½ teaspoon baking powder

1 teaspoon baking soda

2 tablespoons brown sugar, coconut sugar, or
    sugar substitute

2 cups gluten-free flour

For your topping:

¼ cup chocolate chips

Dairy-free option: Use plant milk

Lower-sugar option: Use unsweetened
    plant milk, unsweetened applesauce,
    sugar-free maple syrup, sugar-free
    chocolate chips, and a sugar substitute

Vegan option: Use sugar-free maple syrup
    or agave, plant milk, vegan chocolate
    chips, and make sure your sugar is vegan

When I was a kid, we had dessert every single night in my house. I loved it. As an adult, in my own home, I intend on doing the same. The only difference now is I focus on making healthy dessert treats packed with nutritional benefits. These mini loaves are packed with bananas, apple, and pumpkin puree so you'll be meeting your daily fruit requirement in no time!

What to do:

Preheat oven to 350°F.

Mix wet ingredients together in one medium-sized bowl. Fully combine so there are no lumps and set aside. In a separate medium-sized bowl, mix dry ingredients together. Slowly, add the wet ingredients to the dry bowl, mixing slowly until batter is fully combined and smooth. The batter should resemble the thickness of brownie batter.

Pour into a nonstick, eight-cavity, 15 × 9½–inch mini loaf pan. Fill each cavity approximately one half to three-quarters of the way full. Bake for 30 minutes.

Add chocolate chips on top immediately after removing from the oven so they melt.

To make these a healthy protein treat

Instead of using 2 cups of gluten-free flour, sub 1½ cups of gluten-free flour + ½ cup of protein powder. Cooking time and texture will remain the same.

10 Healthy Mix-and-Match Applesauce Breads

Yield: 6–8 mini loaves

Gluten-free | Vegan
Options: Dairy-free | Lower-sugar | Vegan

What you'll need:

1 mashed banana

1½ cups apple sauce

½ cup maple syrup, honey, or agave

⅓ cup plant-based milk

½ teaspoon baking powder

1 teaspoon baking soda

3 tablespoon brown sugar, coconut sugar, or
   sugar substitute

2 cups gluten-free flour

Dairy-free option: Use plant milk

Lower-sugar option: Use unsweetened
   plant milk, unsweetened applesauce,
   sugar-free maple syrup, and a sugar
   substitute

Vegan option: Use sugar-free maple syrup
   or agave, plant milk, and make sure your
   sugar is vegan. Skip the honey.

This dessert bread is made with hidden mashed bananas and hidden applesauce! This bread has no oil and no butter and is the perfect way to start your day on a healthy note or to end it with a lean dessert.

What to do:

Preheat oven to 350°F.

Mix wet ingredients together in one medium-sized bowl. Fully combine so there are no lumps and set aside. In a separate medium-sized bowl, mix dry ingredients together. Slowly, add the wet ingredients to the dry bowl, mixing slowly until batter is fully combined and smooth. Next, fold in desired mix-in ingredients. The batter should resemble the thickness of brownie batter.

Pour into nonstick, eight-cavity, 15 × 9½–inch mini loaf pan. Fill each cavity approximately one half to three-quarters of the way full. Bake for 30 minutes.

Remove from oven and let sit for 5 minutes before serving. You can store the loaves in an air-tight container in the fridge for 1 to 3 days or in the freezer for up to 3 months. To warm, pop in the microwave in increments of 30 seconds until the loaf reaches desired temperature. Best served warm.

10 Mix-In Combinations to Make This Banana Bread Your Own

Blueberry Cranberry Bread
Mix in ¼ cup blueberries + 3 tablespoons dried cranberries into batter before baking.

Raisin Cinnamon Bread
Mix in ¼ cup of raisins + 3 tablespoons cinnamon into batter before baking.

Matcha Banana Bread
Mix in 3 tablespoons matcha powder into batter before baking.

Toasted Coconut Bread
Add 1 tablespoon shredded coconut flakes on top before baking.

Chocolate Chip Bread
Mix in 3 tablespoons vegan chocolate chips into batter before baking.

Lemon Blueberry Bread
Mix in ¼ cup blueberries + 2 tablespoons lemon juice into batter before baking.

Apple Cinnamon Bread
Mix in ⅓ cup diced apples + 3 tablespoons cinnamon into batter before baking.

Double Chocolate Chip Bread
Mix in ⅓ cup of vegan chocolate chips + 2 tablespoons cocoa powder into batter before baking.

Churro Bread
Mix in 2 tablespoons graduated sugar + 2 tablespoons cinnamon into batter before baking. Sprinkle cinnamon and sugar on top of each loaf before baking.

Peanut Butter Chocolate Chip Bread
Mix in ¼ cup vegan chocolate chips + ¼ cup peanut butter chips before baking. Top each slice with peanut butter when ready to eat!

Healthier Oatmeal Apple Crisp

Yield: 8–10 servings

Gluten-free | Dairy-free | Vegan
Option: Lower-sugar

For your apple base:

14–16 honeycrisp apples

⅓ cup brown sugar, coconut sugar, or sugar
  substitute

2 teaspoons salt

1 tablespoon cinnamon

For your gluten-free crumb topping:

1 cup vegan butter

2 cup gluten-free old-fashioned oats

2 cups gluten-free flour

1 cup brown sugar or coconut sugar

2 tablespoons cinnamon

Lower-sugar option: Use sugar substitute
  instead of sugar

Apple crisp is always the first fall recipe I make to usher in the colder weather. Apple crisps are always packed with cinnamon, butter, and a good crunchy topping. I always want to eat more than just one serving at a time, so I came up with this guilt-free oatmeal apple crisp to ensure you can eat as many servings in one sitting as you want! This recipe uses vegan butter, gluten-free old fashion oats, and gluten-free flour!

What to do:

Preheat oven to 400°F.

On a large cutting board, slice all the apples into ¼-inch slices. Add apple slices to a large mixing bowl. Add brown sugar, salt, and cinnamon. Toss together until apples are fully coated.

Pour apples into a 9 × 13–inch baking dish. I like to use a clear baking dish so you can see the apples baking. This will make it easier to know when the apple crisp is done baking since you will be able to see the apples and butter bubbling below the crumb topping.

In a separate bowl, mix together gluten-free crumb topping ingredients. Mixture should clump together, forming crumbs, and should feel slightly wet to the touch. If it feels too dry, you can add more butter.

Pour crumb mixture over top of apples and bake on 400°F for 45 minutes until you can see the apples and butter bubbling below the crumb topping. Once done baking, remove from oven and let sit for 3 to 5 minutes before serving.

Serve with vegan ice cream or vegan whipped cream!

6 Mix-In Combinations to Make This Apple Crisp Your Own

Chocolate Chip Apple Crisp
Add 2 tablespoons cocoa powder to the crumb mixture. Top apple crisp with ¼ cup vegan chocolate chips before baking.

Blueberry Apple Crisp
Add 1 cup blueberries into the apple mixture before baking.

Strawberry Apple Crisp
Add 1 cup strawberries into the apple mixture before baking.

Red, White, and Blue Crisp
Add ½ cup blueberries and ½ cup strawberries into the apple mixture before baking. Top apple crisp with ¼ cup white chocolate chips before baking.

Peach and Apple Crisp
Use 6 peaches and 6 apples for the base. Add 2 tablespoons of sugar-free maple syrup to the base mixture before baking.

Raisin Cinnamon Apple Crisp
Add 1 cup raisins to the base mixture before baking.

Simple Five-Ingredient Banana Bread

Yield: 1 loaf (8 slices)

Gluten-free | Dairy-free | Vegan
Option: Nut-free

What you'll need:

3 mashed bananas

⅓ cup peanut butter or nut butter

¼–½ cup applesauce

1½ cups gluten-free flour

1 teaspoon baking soda

Nut-free option: Swap out peanut butter for tahini, chickpea butter, or granola butter

This recipe is the perfect base for whatever your favorite flavors are. You can add any toppings or mix-ins you want to this recipe. Want to make it a raisin cinnamon banana bread? Add ½ cup raisins and 3 tablespoons cinnamon. Want to make it a peanut butter chocolate chip banana bread? Use peanut butter and mix in an extra ½ cup of chocolate chips. You can also choose to top each slice as you eat it. I made the base banana bread, then each night for dessert, I microwave my individual slice for 30 seconds and then top with peanut butter, chocolate syrup, caramel, and strawberries.

What to do:

Preheat oven to 350°F.

Mix wet ingredients together in one bowl. Fully combine until it is smooth and there are no lumps. Mix dry ingredients together in another bowl. Slowly add the wet ingredients to the dry bowl. Combine until mixture is smooth like thick cake batter.

Pour into a nonstick loaf pan. Bake for 50 minutes until bread is browned around the edges and pops back up when you lightly push a finger down in the center.

Healthy Double Chocolate Brownie Donuts

Yield: 12 donuts

Gluten-free | Dairy-free | Vegan
Options: Lower-sugar | Nut-free

What you'll need:

2 mashed bananas

½ cup peanut butter, tahini, nut butter,
   chickpea butter, or granola butter

½ cup cocoa powder

¼ cup plant-based milk

1 teaspoon baking powder

¼ cup maple syrup

For your icing:

1 cup chocolate hummus

Lower-sugar option: Use sugar-free maple
   syrup

Nut-free option: Use tahini, chickpea
   butter, or granola butter

These donuts are the perfect healthy weeknight treat! They are made with mashed bananas and without oil and butter. Plus, they're topped with a chocolate hummus icing for a healthy way to satisfy your chocolate craving!

What to do:

Preheat oven to 350°F.

Mix wet ingredients together in one medium-sized bowl. Fully combine so there are no lumps and set aside. In a separate medium-sized bowl, mix dry ingredients together. Slowly, add the wet ingredients to the dry bowl, mixing slowly until batter is fully combined and smooth. The batter should resemble the thickness of brownie batter.

Pour into donut pan. Fill each cavity approximately one half to three-quarters of the way full. Bake for 20 minutes. Remove from oven and let fully cool before icing. Ice with chocolate hummus for a healthy icing option!

Apple Cider Bread

Yield: 1 loaf

Gluten-free | Dairy-free | Nut-free | Vegan
Option: Lower-sugar

What you'll need:

2¼ cups gluten-free flour

¼ cup brown sugar or coconut sugar

¼ cup white granulated sugar or coconut sugar

3 teaspoons baking powder

3 teaspoons apple pie spice

¼ cup applesauce

1 diced apple

1 cup plant-based milk

1 tablespoon apple cider vinegar

Lower-sugar option: Use sugar substitute instead of sugar, use sugar-free applesauce, and unsweetened plant milk

This apple cider bread is made with applesauce and diced apples. It has no oil and no butter, making this the perfect healthy treat for breakfast, brunch, or dessert!

What to do:

Preheat oven to 350°F.

Mix wet ingredients together in one medium-sized bowl. Fully combine so there are no lumps and set aside. In a separate medium-sized bowl, mix dry ingredients together. Slowly, add the wet ingredients to the dry bowl, mixing slowly until batter is fully combined and smooth. The batter should resemble the thickness of brownie batter.

Line a loaf pan with parchment paper for easy removal and easy cleanup! Pour batter into loaf pan. Bake for 60 to 70 minutes. Remove from oven and let fully cool before slicing.

Slices of this bread are best served toasted with vegan butter or peanut butter.

Salted Chocolate and Banana Bread Blondies

Yield: 9 blondies

Gluten-free | Dairy-free | Tree nut–free
Options: Lower-sugar | Nut-free | Vegan

What you'll need:

2 tablespoons plant-based milk

2 mashed bananas

½ cup peanut butter or nut butter

3 tablespoons maple syrup, honey, or agave

½ cup gluten-free flour

¼ cup sugar or coconut sugar

½ teaspoon baking powder

¼ teaspoon baking soda

For your topping:

Sprinkle of sea salt

Vegan or sugar-free chocolate chips

Lower-sugar option: Use sugar substitute instead of sugar and unsweetened plant milk

Nut-free option: Use tahini, chickpea butter, or granola butter

Vegan option: Use plant-based milk and sugar-free maple syrup or agave. Make sure your sugar is vegan.

I love everything about the combination of sea salt and chocolate. I love sweet and salty treats. These blondies are the perfect healthy snack or healthy dessert. They have no oil, no eggs, and no butter, but you'd never know! Packed with banana flavor, and vegan chips, these blondies are the perfect weeknight dessert.

What to do:

Preheat the oven to 350°F.

Mix wet ingredients together in one bowl. Fully combine so there are no lumps. Mix dry ingredients together in another bowl. Slowly add the wet ingredients to the dry bowl. Combine.

Pour into a nonstick 9 × 9–inch baking dish. You can spray the baking dish with light oil spray or line with parchment paper. Bake for 20 to 25 minutes. Remove from the oven. Immediately top with chocolate chips and salt. Let the chocolate chips melt on top. Let cool for 15 minutes before serving.

Chocolate Chip Pancake Bread

Yield: 6–8 mini loaves

Gluten-free | Nut-free
Options: Dairy-free | Lower-sugar | Vegan

What you'll need:

2 cups gluten-free pancake mix

⅔ cup water

½ tablespoon maple syrup

2 tablespoons cocoa powder

2 mashed bananas

2 eggs or vegan egg substitute

¾ cup chocolate chunks

Dairy-free option: Use vegan/dairy-free chocolate chips

Lower-sugar options: Use sugar-free chocolate chips, sugar-free maple syrup, and sugar-free pancake mix

Vegan option: Use vegan egg substitute and vegan chocolate chips

Is it breakfast? Is it dessert? Can it be both?! This double chocolate pancake bread is gluten free, dairy free, has no oil, no butter, and is a perfect healthy option!

What to do:

Preheat the oven to 350°F.

Mix wet ingredients together in one bowl. Fully combine so there are no lumps. Mix dry ingredients together in another bowl. Slowly add the wet ingredients to the dry bowl. Combine and pour into a nonstick loaf pan. You can spray the baking dish with light oil spray or line with parchment paper. Bake for 30 minutes or until the center is set. Remove from the oven. Let cool before serving. Slice and top each slice with peanut butter and extra maple syrup, if desired.

Red Velvet Mini Cupcakes
with Vegan Cream Cheese Frosting

Yield: 24 cupcakes

Gluten-free | Dairy-free | Nut-free
Options: Higher-protein | Lower-sugar | Vegan

What you'll need:

1 cup plant-based milk

2 teaspoons white vinegar

1 cup gluten-free flour

⅓ cup protein powder or more gluten-free flour

¼ cup cornstarch

2 tablespoons cocoa powder

⅔ cup brown sugar or coconut sugar

1 teaspoon baking powder

¼ teaspoon salt

½ cup applesauce

¼ cup tahini

3–5 drops red food coloring

Higher-protein option: Use protein powder option

Lower-sugar option: Use sugar substitute, sugar-free applesauce, and sugar-free plant milk

Vegan option: Use plant-based milk, vegan-friendly sugar, and vegan food coloring

Celebrate Valentine's Day with these mini red velvet cakes. The cake is a healthy dessert option that's actually pretty good for you! They're gluten-free, dairy-free, vegan, and nut-free and are made with applesauce, plant-based milk, and tahini.

What to do:

Preheat the oven to 350°F. Mix wet ingredients together in one bowl. Fully combine so there are no lumps. Mix dry ingredients together in another bowl. Slowly add the wet ingredients to the dry bowl. Mix ingredients and pour into the cupcake tray. Line cupcake cavities or spay with light cooking spray. Bake for 15 to 20 minutes or until the centers are set. Remove from the oven. Let cool before icing.

Three-Ingredient Cream Cheese Frosting

Dairy-free | Gluten-free | Nut-free | Vegan

What you'll need:

½ cup vegan cream cheese

½ cup vegan butter

1 cup powdered sugar or sugar substitute

Shredded coconut, if desired

What to do:

Combine these ingredients together in a medium-sized bowl. Mix until icing is smooth and thick with no lumps. Add to a piping bag and ice each cupcake. Top each cupcake with shredded coconut, if desired.

Chocolate Cupcake Bites

Yield: 24 cupcakes

Gluten-free | Dairy-free | Nut-free
Options: Higher-protein | Lower-sugar | Vegan

What you'll need:

1 cup plant-based milk

2 teaspoons white vinegar

1 cup gluten-free flour

⅓ cup protein powder or more gluten-free flour

¼ cup cornstarch

2 tablespoons cocoa powder

⅔ cup brown sugar or coconut sugar

1 teaspoon baking powder

¼ teaspoon salt

½ cup applesauce

¼ cup tahini

Higher-protein option: Use protein powder option

Lower-sugar option: Use sugar substitute, sugar-free applesauce, and sugar-free plant milk

Vegan option: Use plant-based milk and vegan-friendly sugar

They're low in fat, high in protein, and a healthy dessert option that's actually pretty good for you! They're gluten-free, dairy-free, vegan, and nut-free and are made with applesauce, plant-based milk, and tahini.

What to do:

Preheat the oven to 350°F.

Mix wet ingredients together in one bowl. Fully combine so there are no lumps. Mix dry ingredients together in another bowl. Slowly add the wet ingredients to the dry bowl. Mix ingredients and pour into the cupcake tray. Line cupcake cavities or spay with light cooking spray, if desired.

Bake for 15 to 20 minutes or until the centers are set. Remove from the oven. Let cool before icing. Top with icing, peanut butter, tahini, chocolate sauce, whipped cream, or berries!

Everything-but-the-Kitchen-Sink Brownies

Yield: 9 brownies

Gluten-free

Options: Dairy-free | Higher-protein | Lower-sugar | Nut-free | Vegan

For your base:

¼ cup gluten-free flour

¼ cup protein powder or more gluten-free flour

¼ cup sugar, coconut sugar, or sugar substitute

½ teaspoon baking powder

¼ teaspoon baking soda

2 tablespoons plant-based milk

1 cup mashed bananas (approximately 2 bananas)

½ cup peanut butter or nut butter

3 tablespoons maple syrup

For your topping:

1 cup chocolate chips

⅓ cup shredded coconut

1 tablespoon sea salt

What you'll need after baking:

¼ cup chocolate syrup

¼ cup caramel sauce

I'm a firm believer that you should have dessert every day, especially These Everything-but-the-Kitchen-Sink Brownies! They are gluten-free and topped with vegan chocolate and shredded toasted coconut. They're oil-free, have no butter, and are a great healthy dessert option.

What to do:

Preheat the oven to 350°F.

Mix wet ingredients together in one bowl. Fully combine so there are no lumps. Mix dry ingredients together in another bowl. Slowly add the wet ingredients to the dry bowl. Combine and pour into a nonstick 9 × 9–inch baking dish. You can spray the baking dish with light oil spray or line with parchment paper.

Add chocolate chips, shredded coconut, and sea salt on top. Do not mix in.

Bake for 20 to 25 minutes. Remove from the oven. Immediately top with chocolate chips and salt. Let the chocolate chips melt on top. Let cool for 15 minutes before serving. Once cooled, top with chocolate syrup and caramel sauce.

Dairy-free option: Top with vegan/dairy-free chocolate sauce and vegan/dairy-free caramel sauce. Use vegan/dairy-free chocolate chips.

Higher-protein option: Use protein powder option

Lower-sugar option: Use sugar substitute, sugar-free plant milk, sugar-free maple syrup, and sugar-free chocolate chips

Nut-free option: Use tahini, chickpea butter, or granola butter

Vegan option: Top with vegan chocolate sauce and vegan caramel sauce. Use vegan chocolate chips.

Make Your Own Dessert Board

Yield: 1 dessert board

Gluten-free
Options: Dairy-free | Low-carb | Low-fat | Nut-free | Vegan

I am a huge fan of charcuterie boards, and since they're such a big hit at any get together, why not translate it to dessert?

These boards are a really easy way to have a little something for everyone. I like to include vegan options, such as vegan chocolate or fruit. I include dairy-free options, such as chocolate hummus and gluten-free pretzels. I like to make sure there's fresh fruit available for anyone watching their sugar intake or fat intake.

You can really put anything on the dessert board, but I like to break up my dessert boards into a chocolate section, a crunchy section, a snack section, and a healthy option section.

For your sweet section:

Dairy-free chocolate bars with peanuts (pictured here)

Chocolate-covered gluten-free pretzels

Chocolate-covered banana slices

Mini gluten-free brownie bites

Chocolate-covered strawberries

For your crunchy section:

Gluten-free chocolate chip cookies (pictured here)

Gluten-free mini granola bars (pictured here)

Candied nuts or candied grapes

Popcorn or caramel popcorn

For your snack section:

Crunchy mini chocolate rice cakes (pictured here)

Sweet and salty crispy corn or crispy chickpeas (pictured here)

Dairy-free chocolate chips

Gluten-free pretzels

For your healthy option section:

Chocolate hummus (pictured here)

Dried pineapple slices (pictured here)

Dried banana slices

Yogurt-covered gluten-free pretzels

Strawberries

Blueberries

See following page to put a holiday spin on these dessert boards!

For a Holiday Spin, Try These

These dessert boards are perfect for wowing a crowd on a holiday! You can change up the ingredients to more festive options! For Valentine's Day, you can use all chocolate and red treats. For Halloween, you can use all chocolate and orange treats. And for Chistmas, use red and green!

Valentine's Day
Choose all chocolate treats and red treats. For instance, chocolates, gluten-free brownies, strawberries, raspberries, chocolate-covered berries, etc.

Fourth of July
Choose all red, white, and blue treats. For instance, strawberries, blueberries, white chocolate–covered berries, white chocolate, white yogurt–covered pretzels, etc.

Halloween
Choose all the dark chocolate and orange treats: dark chocolate candy bars, any kind of mini candy bars you'd hand out for Halloween, brown and orange M&M's, chocolate-covered orange slices, etc.

Thanksgiving
Choose all brown and orange treats. For instance, gluten-free brownies, gluten-free chocolate chip cookies, chocolates, chocolate-covered orange slices, dried pineapple, dried banana chips, etc.

Christmas
Choose all the red and green treats: strawberries, raspberries, white yogurt–dipped pretzels with red and green sprinkles, red and green M&M's, etc.

Acknowledgments

Writing a cookbook is a funny thing. You already know all your favorite recipes by heart, and to you it's a given which recipes you want to share, but there's an entire team in place focused on getting those recipes, your recipes, from your heart to the page in a way I never imagined was possible. I first want to say thank you to my literary agent, Joseph Perry, who took a chance on me during a global pandemic when I had no blog and barely enough Instagram followers to matter. He believed in me and saw the potential of my photos and my recipes, and that has changed everything. I want to thank Nicole Frail and Nicole Mele for making my cookbook vision come to life seamlessly. I want to thank everyone behind the scenes at Skyhorse Publishing who worked tirelessly to make my cookbook dreams into a reality, and my publicist, Carrie Bachman, for all the hard work she put into making this cookbook a success.

Aside from my publishing team, I want to thank Andrew, my fiancé, for putting up with me endlessly directing the way he cooks so it looks good in a photo or in a video, for doing thousands of dishes behind the scenes of these very photos in this book, for taste testing all the recipes that did make it into the book, and an even bigger thank you for taste testing the recipes that didn't make the book. But above all, I want to thank him for being the biggest fan of my whole life.

I want to take the time to thank my friends for not only putting up with my endlessly evolving food allergy situation over the past decade, but also for their unwavering quest to find the best gluten-free, nut-free, and dairy-free options in any city we are in. From New York City to Hoboken to Jamaica to even the allergy-friendly recipes they make at their own houses when I come over, I cannot say thank you enough for always creating a safe space for me to feel comfortable eating.

And lastly to my family. To my parents, my sister, and my in-laws. For all the menus you've had to stalk for me, for all the gluten-free dishes you've made on holidays for me, and how accommodating you've been at every social event, holiday, and family party with me, I love you all.

Index